LOVE THERAPY

Love

Therapy

PAUL · D · MORRIS

TYNDALE HOUSE PUBLISHERS, INC.
WHEATON, ILLINOIS

COVERDALE HOUSE PUBLISHERS LTD.
LONDON, ENGLAND

Library of Congress Catalog Card Number 74-80151. ISBN 8423-3860-8 cloth; 8423-3861-6 paper. Copyright © 1974 Tyndale House Publishers, Inc., Wheaton, Illinois. All rights reserved. First printing, June 1974. Printed in the United States of America

For
Claud Joseph Smithson, III
In memoriam

CONTENTS

PART 1

Reclaiming a Prerogative

INTRODUCTION: SPEAKING PERSONALLY

Although my father was a Baptist minister, I did not become properly related to God until I was twenty years of age. The minister of a rural church in Oklahoma, he died while I was still in infancy. My mother was left with five children including me, only a few months old. The parents and family of both my father and mother lived hundreds of miles away in Georgia—they may as well have lived thousands. Travel in 1937 was difficult even for the well-to-do. We were poor. My father was often paid in produce or labor. But with the help of the families in Georgia, my mother took her children to Atlanta.

Mother had suffered much as all of us had, really. But somehow children readjust more rapidly and learn to adapt to the realities of living with only slightly dented optimism. Mother was not nearly so shielded. Combined with recent traumatic birth complications, the death of her husband, and financial destitution, the pressure was enough to render her mentally irresponsible. She was committed to the state hospital.

A decision was made to keep the children together (a decision for which I am grateful to my parents' families), and so my widowed aunt on my mother's side moved in with us. I grew up during the war years with Germany and Japan. We had only the money of the combined salaries of my aunt and my oldest sister. My older two brothers and sisters contributed as the years went on. Somehow, through it all, we managed to escape the welfare rolls. I guess we were too proud for that sort of thing.

During these years we made periodic trips to Millegeville, 100 miles away, to see Mother. These trips left an indelible impression on my young mind. The hospital reeked with urine and alcohol. I imagined people caged, beating their heads against padded walls and shrieking howls of mental agony. The old female patients in the hospital halls where we waited for Mother to be delivered would stare at me. Some would smile. Some would frown. Some would simply sit on hard-backed benches and rock back and forth, staring into some dim memory of childhood.

It was a shattering blow to a proud child to think that his mother was like this. She never really seemed to be. But she was there just the same. The enjoyable part came when we would take her on outings into the bright Georgia sunshine. There was a barbecue-type restaurant nearby where we could picnic on tables among the pines. The management kept an animal pen where I usually found a raccoon or monkey or squirrels. Mother would talk with her brothers and sisters, and I would wonder whether or not she knew me or loved me. But it was beautiful; that is, until the time came for her to go back to the hospital.

Mother never resisted. She always wanted to "come home." She never did. She stayed there twenty-five years, until she died with a malignant tumor.

Now, I am convinced that Mother's long hospitalization was not necessary. All during my childhood, which comprised the major portion of that twenty-five years, Mother was never that "sick." We were often told she could come home if we could hire a practical nurse to stay with her, but we were too poor for that. Later, when she had been there too long "for it to matter," we reasoned that she was happier there than she'd be if brought home to unfamiliar surroundings. Whether or not this would have, in fact, been the case was never tested.

Not only was the economic factor for the lack of my mother's mental rehabilitation not that overpoweringly prohibitive, but I believe she didn't receive proper therapy. This is even a more compelling reason for her tragedy. It isn't that the doctors weren't conscientious or that they were incompetent. I have no reason to believe that the physicians who treated her didn't go out of their way and perhaps even beyond themselves to help her. The nurses and aides seemed to treat her with respect and dignity. Everything possible was being done to make her "as comfortable as possible." The years passed. She grew old, and I grew up.

1

THE LIMITS OF PSYCHIATRY: A CHALLENGE TO CHRISTIANS

Thousands of people are sequestered in our mental institutions today, who could have been out years ago leading productive and rewarding lives. The science of psychiatry is simply inefficient. The greatest testimony to this fact is the number of "incurables" it cannot seem to help. Even milder neuroses when subjected to psychiatric therapy are often worsened. To be sure, there have been successes. The study and practice of psychiatry and psychology is most certainly valid, but it is limited in what it can do.

This limitation stems mainly from the fact that the therapy can address itself only to a "part" of the total person. That is, it treats the body and the soul in some measured degree, but it cannot treat and in many cases does not even recognize the *spirit* of man. If Scripture is to be trusted, we are forced to conclude that man has a spirit. And we must conclude that he is influenced by it.

However, I do not agree with many that the human spirit is "the most important part" of man. I think it is a mistake to elevate the importance of the heart over the brain, or an arm over a leg, or the soul over the spirit, or the spirit over the body. Man may be a tripartite creature, but he is *one* man. He is one entity and must be treated as such. When one part is sick, the whole is affected.

This world is full of deep, probing human trauma. Men and women simply have never adjusted to the "curse." We never will. The reason that physicians exist is to help us live with and in spite of our disease, our destructive impulses, and our hostile world. As a minister of the gospel, it is my responsibility to bring men and women to God, or, stated differently, to bring God to them. So my ministry and my therapy are directed to the whole individual— body, soul, and spirit. The psychologist, the man of medicine, the Christian minister: each of us has basically the same goal—to help. It is tragic that these three "scientific" disciplines, while following the trichotomy of man, fail in their efforts to function as one—as man does.

People's problems are, more often than not, tied together. That mental stress is the origin of more than eighty percent of all bodily ills is no secret statistic. If this is true, why aren't ministers more involved in the healing process?

I think the answer to this question, while complex and cloudy, is best seen in the structure of the professional establishment.

This structure is not one of organization, but one of philosophy. It is so strong, however, that it is used as a criterion for state law. It is a structure combining medicine and psychology to the exclusion of religion. This, of course, generally excludes biblical truth and its practice as well. Many states, among them California, do not recognize ministers as expert in the field of correcting aberrant human behavior. They do not even license them as qualified marriage counselors. The requirements for such a license call for academic programs outside the average minister's sphere of training. These academic programs are designed by those already in the psychiatric field, themselves the product of this self-perpetuating grist mill. God is not presented or even given serious thought by this incredibly exclusivist circle of professional self-preservation. Yet the state recognizes this circle as the only source of competent criteria upon which to formulate the law governing the healing of men's souls. One cannot help but commend the reason for the existence of such requirements, but by their very nature they exclude from state licensing very competent counselors.

In addition to the state's contribution to the "structure," the professions themselves prescribe exclusive atmosphere. It is not uncommon to find a helpless minister who, having encountered a problem he "can't handle," refers his client to a "professional." The minister isn't entirely to blame for his inferior attitude. The state and the professions involved have gotten the message through to him that he is not trained to treat problems of the mind. He had better content himself with "spiritual" problems. He must leave the soul to the more competent hands of the psychologist. In the spirit of meekness, the lowly minister has abdicated one of the most vital responsibilities that God gave him. What he doesn't realize is that, so far as healing effectiveness is concerned, irrespective of the posture of the state or the professional attitude of the psychologist, he is at least on a par with his "professional" counterpart and in many cases is superior to him. In order to be fair we hasten to add that, in many instances, a properly trained Christian psychologist or psychiatrist is more competent than an ill-equipped minister. Perhaps it would be wise at this point to suggest what is meant by a "properly trained Christian psychologist."

Any believing psychologist or psychiatrist whose therapy is based upon a Christian orientation is to that degree, in my opinion, properly trained. However, it would be still better if one could be found who, in addition to his psychiatric training, had obtained a divinity degree from a theologically conservative seminary and who had accumulated two years' experience on at least the associate pastor level of a local church. I am speaking here, of course, of those who have chosen counseling and psychiatric therapy as a profession.

What we need to realize is:

(1) The most effective body of *therapeutic truth* this planet has ever seen is provided in that Book most ministers spent three years absorbing in rigorous academic effort—after finishing university training. For some of us, the time and effort have been even longer.

(2) Along with his ministry of preaching, the responsibility of a pastor is to *"counsel paracaletically."* Contact with people in trouble in the sequestered halls of the clinic or counseling office is one thing. Empathizing with people's agony in the ghetto or when a child dies, providing counsel prior to marriage or in any of the

countless "laboratory experiences" that are part of the everyday lives of most pastors are quite another.

(3) Too many of us have ruled out or minimized the counseling ministry in favor of what I call the *"executive syndrome."* This is another way of saying that some of us enjoy being the chief executive so much that we have little time left over for one-to-one contact with the man in the pew. Some of us would do well to feel for the pulse of a man like young John Witmer, who was a Wheaton College student when he wrote these lines:

> you followers of the Bearded Christ
> and you of the Carpenter
> and you of the Twelve-year Philosopher
> withhold your talk at Easter-Christmasers
>   you back-rowers, and morning onlys
>   and 5 days of chapel already.
> fighters for ecumenical support of Indian Bill 12
> unprejudiced suburbanite who's never eaten chili
> seekers of Truth and Life and The Way,
> PLEASE LISTEN!
> when you
> retreat from your Crusades
> and pull back from your Causes
> and finally have time for somebody,
> have time for me;
> I need somebody to love me.[1]

(4) *People and their problems are the business of Christians.* If God was concerned about the human predicament enough to sacrifice his Son, and to provide an inspired record of his solutions to human problems, it seems reasonable for this to be our focus as well. We must remember that God is concerned with the *whole man,* not just with his spirit. The Bible gives us abundant information, not about setting broken bones or the like, but about healing the non-material wounds of God's highest order of creation. For us to give this responsibility to men and women who aren't even

1. John Witmer, *Rappings,* compiled by Robert Webber (Wheaton: Tyndale House Publishers, 1971).

acquainted with God (indeed to many who consider God a fabrication) is the apex of irresponsibility and incompetence.

Therefore, it is the purpose of the remainder of this book to do two things:

(1) *To provide a challenge to "restructure the Christian mind."* I find it incredible that so many of the tenets held by men and women of faith are not based on scriptural evidence, but on puritan tradition. (It may come as a surprise to some, but the two aren't equal!) This unfortunate situation contributes to psychological problems, not to speak of healing them. Much of Christianity today is a religion of cliches, slogans, and medieval theology. It's no wonder that psychologists look down their noses at us and consider us incompetent—since, to the degree that these things influence us, we are!

(2) *To provide a workable procedure in biblical therapeutic technique.* This should prove valuable to pastors and Christian counselors, as well as to Christian men and women in need of practical, psychologically sound guidance for their own lives and for the lives of others around them.

PART II
Therapeutic Philosophy

2

WHO IS COMPETENT TO COUNSEL?

Who is really competent to counsel? This to me is a critical question. I concede that all of us exercise to a greater or lesser degree some influence over each other. Whether that influence is constructive or destructive is another matter entirely. So, some might argue that the greater the specific training of the person who influences, the greater his field of influence. Particularly, one might add, is this true of those who desire to help others fulfill their potential of happiness and accomplishment. This is the role of a therapist, whether psychiatrist, psychologist, or minister.

Does it necessarily follow that because a person fills a professional role he or she is competent to counsel another? Is training the only or even an adequate prerequisite? I don't think I'm being unfair when I say that the entire psychiatric community would agree, with little qualification, that the answer to both of these questions is yes. That qualification might be that the therapist must be a responsible, well-adjusted personality. I believe that such a position is wrong.

Some ministers believe that their seminary training provides adequate background and qualification for counseling. Thus, Jay Adams rather boldly and perhaps naively remarks, "A good seminary education rather than medical school or a degree in clinical psychology, is the most fitting background for a counselor."[1] In a measure, I would agree with Adams's statement; that is, if I had to make a choice between the two. However, simply to write off the knowledge gained by the study of human behavior as well as certain therapeutic techniques derived from that knowledge (and proved pragmatic by experimentation) seems, in a word, gross.

The point is, no matter how valid or important one's educational background, it is not the critical factor. Technical knowledge is vital, but not absolutely critical. A competent counselor must "know the message as well as the man," but there is something beyond this. A therapist may be thoroughly versed in psychology, medicine, and the Scripture. He may be well-adjusted and responsible. He may even genuinely desire to serve mankind. But unless he possesses something else, his counseling therapy will be inadequate, ineffective, and incompetent.

Adams suggests that in addition to goodness and knowledge, the competent counselor must possess wisdom. He defines wisdom as "the skillful use of divine truth for God's glory."[2] This is a fine statement, and I will certainly not attempt to deny its veracity. A man may be able to use divine truth skillfully for God's glory, however, and still be a poor counselor. What is it, then, that is the final catalyst? What is it that in and of itself alone provides for competence in counseling? *It is a gift: a spiritual, charismatic gift.*

It is wrong to conclude that all Christians, given proper understanding of the Scripture, are competent to counsel. And here, of course, is where I depart sharply from Adams's nouthetic approach to counseling. (The word "nouthetic" is Adams's English adjective form of the Greek verb *noutheteo,* usually translated "admonish" or "warn," as in Romans 5:14; Colossians 1:28; and 1 Thessalonians 5:12, 14.[3]) That counseling is one of the eighteen

1. Jay E. Adams, *Competent to Counsel* (Philadelphia: Presbyterian and Reformed Publishing Company, 1970), p. 61.
2. *Ibid.,* p. 62.
3. *Ibid.,* p. 41.

or so "spiritual gifts" is to me not a debatable matter. And God has not given every believer this gift any more than he has given each believer the gift of "tongues" or of "pastor-teacher."

I know people who have never been to seminary and yet possess this gift. I wouldn't be afraid to trust these people with my mother or even the worst "incurable" psychotic. These are the most competent counselors in the world. The most eminent psychiatrist without this gift would do well to learn from the lowliest believer who possesses it. These men and women have been given *supernatural ability* by God, which they did not possess before he gave it.

Having said this, I want to say that the gift of counseling is not confined to relatively few people. It is widespread. I want to say further, that training in the Scripture and in the science of applied psychology greatly enhances the effectiveness of someone with this gift. The more a person knows, the more that gift can be used.

It is not difficult to discover whether or not you have the gift of counseling. (1) You must understand that spiritual *gifts are given for the edification* or the health of the church and its individual members. Spiritual gifts are to be distinguished from natural talents, in that many nonbelievers possess talents. Any one who is not a Christian cannot possess a spiritual gift. This is the problem with the psychological community as a whole. Their therapeutic system is based upon a humanistic philosophy. Just as a man is incomplete without God's gift of eternal life, their therapy is incomplete and inadequate without God's spiritual gift.

(2) *You must desire the gift of counseling.* I know no one with this gift who finds dissatisfaction in helping others with their problems. On the other hand, plenty of people don't genuinely want to involve themselves with people and their problems. The school of philosophic thought which maintains that the therapist should establish a professional detachment from his counselee bears testimony either to ignorance, bad judgment, or lack of sincerity and desire to help—and thus lack of this gift. To desire it does not mean that you necessarily must beg God for it. I simply mean that you must view helping people in this manner as a desirable personal goal for yourself.

(3) Having satisfied these requirements, as a prospective therapist you must *train yourself* to the best of your abilities and re-

sources. Success in this will strongly indicate the validity of your gift.

(4) You must *try it*. You need not wait until you have trained yourself academically before you try to help someone by counseling. Sometimes men and women discover that they have the gift of counseling by virtue of the fact that others begin to come to them for help.

(5) You may safely assume that God has given you the spiritual gift of counseling *if your efforts produce positive, constructive results*. Results like these may not always be observable, but generally they are. The real test is made in the crucible of experience. Is there substantial success in your work? If the answer is affirmative, then your gift becomes obvious. By *success* is meant a specific change in personality, not simply symptomatic relief. The testimony of those in a position to observe you will be an additional indicator of the genuineness of your gift. If others can see evidence of proven ability, then you may conclude that it is indeed there.

Being gifted spiritually, while a supernatural imposition, is really not "mysterious" or esoteric. All you need to do is pursue your desires, and if they materialize substantially, then you have discovered the gift ("ability") which has led to your success.

3

REALITY THERAPY

One of the most revolutionary concepts of psychiatry to come along in a long time is the therapeutic approach known as Reality Therapy. Dr. William Glasser has developed the concept, which is based upon three tenets of therapeutic philosophy: (1) Involvement, (2) Responsibility, (3) Right and Wrong.

In preparation for the presentation of Reality Therapy in this book, I interviewed Dr. Richard M. Hawes, a practicing psychologist who is vice-president of the Institute for Reality Therapy. Salient points of this interview (summarized here) reveal the philosophy and procedure of this revolutionary technique:

Morris: Dr. Hawes, exactly what is Reality Therapy?

Hawes: Reality Therapy is built upon a relationship between two people. It is a congenial, mutually understanding, warm relationship. This relationship is called "Involvement." Without it, Reality Therapy cannot effectively function. Likewise, it is the most difficult part of the process. Many patients distrust the therapist or transfer their hostility toward him. This defeats our purpose. Often the most lengthy portion of therapy is taken up in the establishment of involvement. Once one becomes involved, once the therapist and his viewpoints are important to the patient and have positive influence with him, responsible behavior is detailed. That is, the patient is helped to understand the difference between irresponsible and responsible behavior. Then the process of rejecting irresponsible behavior and encouraging responsibility is begun. Once the therapist has established involvement, he has won the right to guide, or at least his guidance is then accepted by the patient. Perhaps it is not quite this structured, but these generally are the areas covered.

Morris: How do you apply Reality Therapy in order to get a person to respond responsibly?

Hawes: By involvement. After the patient views me as someone who is important to him and realizes that likewise he is important to me, he will accept my guidance. When he sees that while I reject his irresponsible behavior I yet accept him as a worthwhile person, he will begin to respond responsibly.

Morris: Do you moralize and give advice?

Hawes: I try to help the patient distinguish between acceptable and unacceptable behavior, but I moralize and advise very little.

Morris: As a professional psychologist, do you endorse the concept of sin?

Hawes: To a degree. To the extent that one infringes upon the rights and liberties of another.

Morris: To what extent do you use CPI, MMPI, Luscher's color test, or other psychological testing?

Hawes: I do not use them at all. And this was my major academic interest.

Morris: How, then, do you approach diagnosis and how much time do you give to it?

Hawes: I do not give any time to it any more. Now my focus is turned toward relating to the patient. When involvement is accomplished, assuming I am a responsible person, this relationship will build him toward that responsibility. Involvement is the key factor in Reality Therapy. It renders diagnosis non-essential.

[*I have reservations about this. Personally, I cannot escape the concept that in order to help someone, I must know what is wrong, and I must know the patient himself. It seems to me that involvement is built upon such mutual knowledge.*]

Morris: To what extent do you employ a psychological vocabulary in describing the various nuances and distinctives of human behavior?

Hawes: I do not use these terms at all, and especially not to my patients. They are dangerous in the sense that when a label is attached to a patient, he invariably accepts the label as an excuse to condone his behavior. He begins to play the role of the label.

Morris: Do you attach significant value to group therapy, and how do you compare it to a one-to-one technique?

Hawes: Yes, definitely. But one-to-one is most important. Even in groups one-to-one is attempted. Group therapy provides an atmosphere of peer acceptance, while irresponsibility is openly and frankly criticized.

Morris: What do you think of "team counseling"? In other words, where two or more counselors attempt to treat the same patient at the same time—the patient is confronted with a group of professionals.

Hawes: I think it is exceptionally poor. It is a colossal "put down" experience for the patient.

[*Obviously, Mr. Hawes had not read Jay Adams' book, where Adams suggests this as an effective method. I agree completely with Hawes in this matter. How could a patient possibly feel at ease in expressing himself in such a situation? To me, this is the most incredible* faux pas *in Adams' system. The absurdity of the thing is illustrated in the experience of Job and his three "friends."*][1]

Morris: Do you attach significant value to sensitivity training?

Hawes: I think there is value in a tactile relationship, yes. However, this is one of the minuses with American culture for the most part. We have a "don't touch me" complex. To be touched is a necessary part of infancy, and I believe it is healthy for adulthood also.

Morris: Do you attach significant value to Freud's procedure of psychoanalysis or to the Rogerian nondirective technique?

Hawes: Not too much. I heard Rogers in San Diego and my evaluation was that he had moved from his former nondirective approach. He is definitely more directive now. With regard to Freud, I do not believe that investigation into the past provides us with a particularly valuable therapeutic tool. The practice of allowing a patient to transfer his problems to some character in his past is valueless.

Morris: Do you reject without qualification the concept of nonorganic mental illness?

Hawes: Carefully. One cannot flippantly overthrow the establishment without cause for regret; but basically I view mental illness as occurring in varying degrees of irresponsibility. This is not to deny that irresponsibility caused by brain damage, etc., is real.

Morris: How do you explain the successful results of conventional therapy and why is Reality Therapy superior?

Hawes: Has conventional therapy succeeded? I would have to challenge that. Reality Therapy is superior because it works. It does succeed.

Morris: Is there sustained value to shock therapy?

1. *Ibid.,* p. 204.

Hawes: No. And the dangers are frightening. It does seem to be effective in some cases but it has never been curative. No one seems to know exactly how it works, but the results of the overload placed upon the electric sensitivity of the central nervous system are almost always dramatic, and not always positive. It is simply the process of passing an electric current through the brain of the patient.

Morris: Dr. Hawes, what are the prospects, in your opinion, for conventional psychiatry as the future unfolds?

Hawes: The established program is self-perpetuating. It will always be around. Reality Therapy represents no threat to them because too many people need help and will pay them $50 or more an hour. They have a great thing going.

This interview with Dr. Hawes was lengthy and informative. His remarks have been condensed and abbreviated here, as he often took considerable time in answering each question. I am deeply grateful for his help. I am not willing, at this point, to accept all of the tenets of Reality Therapy, but I want to say that I am enthusiastic about its effectiveness. Moreover, I firmly believe that the concepts of Involvement, Responsibility, and Right and Wrong are biblical concepts, and are the *right* therapeutic concepts in counseling or deeper treatment of mental illness (or shall I say "irresponsible behavior"?).

4

LOVE THERAPY

Everything said up to this point has now brought us to "ground zero" of what I feel to be the right approach to all nonphysiological human problems. What follows is the essence, the core of the spiritual gift of counseling.

Just before Jesus left this planet he made one of his most significant remarks. He said,

> A new commandment I give unto you . . . as I have loved you . . . ye also love one another. By this shall all men know that ye are my disciples . . . *(John 13:34, 35).*

The uniqueness of this remark is that Jesus spoke of this commandment as being *new.* Yet the command to love is nothing new: it was incorporated into the Mosaic law. The new dimension that gives this commandment a whole new complexion is the statement, "as I have loved you." The most incredible demonstration that Jesus loves me is the fact that he has *involved* himself with me. The story is told that while theologian Karl Barth was lecturing in the

United States a student asked him, "Dr. Barth, what is the most profound thought you have ever had?" Barth thought a moment before he responded. The students probably expected some highly detailed theological discourse, but he answered, "Jesus loves me, this I know, for the Bible tells me so."

Jesus was God. He could have enjoyed whatever it is that God enjoys without ever giving man a thought. But instead, motivated by love, he became a man. How much more involved could he be? He who was and is God, became man. By doing so, he came to know experientially what men know. He experienced heartaches, joys, and temptations as any human would experience them. His suffering was human suffering—to an infinite degree. He loved man enough to become a man. Jesus has said that *I must love,* therefore, *as he loves.*

Moreover, when he left, he sent the Holy Spirit to continue this relationship of involvement with men. He even named the Holy Spirit the Paraclete: One "called alongside." Our therapy is expressed in the same word, *paracaleo,* which is the word used in Romans 12:6–8 for the charismatic gift of "counseling":

> Having then gifts that differ according to the grace that is given to us . . . whether prophecy . . . ministry . . . teaching, or he who . . . *paraklon,* in his *paraklasei* (counseling).

Justification for translating this word in this way is seen in the role of the Holy Spirit himself. He is involved with us. He comforts and guides us. He does not sympathize with wrong behavior, but he does empathize. He is there with us in it, giving us the power to overcome it.

(The word itself is translated variously to mean, to make a request [beseech], to exhort, and to comfort. The word carries with it the basic intent of encouragement, consolation, and comfort. *In this sense* it is used to indicate the *nature* of the vast portion of what preaching or exhortation should be as well. I think it is a mistake, however, to understand the word as used in this passage to mean only preaching as such. Preaching is itself a gift from God as is clearly stipulated in 1 Peter 4:10, 11).

If we understand *counseling* as that process by which one through verbal interaction brings along another to a position of responsibility and mental and spiritual health, then it is the word that most aptly describes the ministry of the Holy Spirit within us. (I do not intend to imply that the Holy Spirit articulates audibly, except by the expression of revealed Truth through believers with the gift of counseling. The gifted believer is to give objective expression through his words and life of this aspect of the Spirit's ministry. The same is obviously true for any charismatic gift. The Christian gift of counseling, therefore, will result in the therapist's "acting out" in words and deeds the paracaletic promptings of the Spirit.)

An effective counselor, then, must develop a genuine relationship of loving involvement with his counselee. He must never be condemnatory (the Spirit of God never condemns a believer), but he must not accept poor performance either. He must guide the counselee by subtle and overt encouragement into responsible behavior. He must help him to understand what it is that God really wants of him, and to distinguish that from what he may think God requires of him.

LEVELS OF RESPONSIBILITY

In Christian terms, what is meant by responsibility? I think we all have a general idea of responsible behavior. But when we interject the Christian component, responsibility assumes the stance of what is responsible for the Christian. When I use the term Christian responsibility, I mean it to be synonymous with Christian maturity. Since this is an equally vague term to most of us, let me say that I consider spirituality and Christian maturity to be separate and distinct. A very young Christian may be spiritual (controlled by the Spirit), but he certainly is not a mature Christian. By *mature* is meant the ingesting and incorporation of biblical truth into life and its proper understanding and application to experience. By this code as well, a person may have been a Christian for forty years and still be immature or irresponsible. Also, sometimes events in life so strongly affect a mature Christian that he begins to act in an immature or irresponsible way.

It is the mission of the Christian therapist to help the believer toward his goal of conformity to the image of Christ, or if he is not

a believer, to help him to come to know those things about God
that will help him to believe. I do not mean by this to present a
short course in Christian evidences and apologetics. *A nonbeliever
must know that God loves because the therapist loves.* On this basis
it is almost inevitable that when involvement is achieved, involvement with God is achieved. If it is not, the Christian therapist must
do what he can for the patient to help him cope with a life that will
never satisfy him completely.

Fundamental to the progressive achievement of acceptable levels
of responsibility is a consistent stabilized pattern of growth toward
the perfection of Christ. In the development of this pattern, all of
us have basic elemental needs which must be fulfilled. They may
vary slightly according to the "authority" one consults, but generally, they include: the need to love and be loved; the need for sexual
satisfaction; the need for environmental security; the need for self-
expression and accomplishment; and (one that you will not find in
psychology texts) the need for reconcilement with God. These
needs are basic to the functional human. In order to meet and fulfil
these needs, Love Therapy projects seven levels of responsibility:

(1) *Basic belief in God.* This is the first intellectual and emotional function that any fulfilled personality must have. Man's need
for God is more basic than his need for sex or food. The unique
thing about this particular need is that it may be almost totally
suppressed throughout life. But the result of this suppression is
never a well-balanced, fulfilled personality. The end result is, of
course, eternally disastrous.

(2) *Basic love for God.* It is impossible for a man to love God
if he is not convinced that God loves him. Love for God is a
criterion for responsible adjustment to life and its complexities. It
is possible, however—indeed it often occurs—for a man to believe
in God, be convinced that God loves him, give intellectual consent
to his love for God, and still not genuinely love him.

(3) *Basic commitment to God.* Each of these levels of responsibility is essential to healthy Christian experience. One may well
think that if this is true, very few Christians are healthy and well
adjusted. I won't offer judgment about that, but it is a fact that
many believers have yet to commit their total life experience to
Christ. Paul says:

I urge *(parakaleo)* you therefore, brethren, by the mercies of God, to present your bodies a living and holy sacrifice, acceptable to God, which is your spiritual service of worship. And do not be conformed to this world, but be transformed by the renewing of your mind, that you may prove what the will of God is, that which is good, and acceptable and perfect *(Romans 12:1, 2, NASB)*.

Note that commitment of this sort results in a transformation of the *mind*. The essential character of this commitment cannot be ignored by the Christian therapist.

Here the phrase "be not conformed to this world" occurs, so perhaps something should be said about *worldliness*. This is rather a worn term, used in fundamentalist vernacular to denote anything that could be conceived of as secular or as belonging to the world as distinct from heaven. We cannot deny that Satan has been given certain latitude in world affairs. But we must not forget that this world and this age belong to God. The cosmos, time, and eternity belong to God—not to Satan. The evil aspect of the world is that part of the cosmos that God has permitted Satan to influence. Therefore, for a believer to be "worldly" is simply another way of saying that he is influenced by evil. He is exploited by satanic pressure as he operates in the context of the cosmos. The opposite must be true of the well-adjusted believer: he must "exploit" instead of being exploited; he must influence instead of being influenced. God made the world. The believer then is to enjoy what God has made and to influence it and control it for good. He is the *salt* of the earth.

(4) *Basic concept of self.* In addition to the above levels, which form one's concept of God, the well-adjusted believer must have an adequate concept of himself. He must be brought out of the degrading, self-negating type of mentality which many Christians believe is the teaching of Jesus and others in Scripture. The believer must view himself as important to God and to others. He must realize that he is needed and that the present world would be incomplete without him. God loves him. God died for him. The believer must develop self-love.

(5) *Basic love for others.* The believer must also develop love for those outside the vertical relationship between himself and God.

The unique aspect of Jesus' new commandment was that we are to love "as he loved us." One cannot escape the fact that Jesus loved with more than the modern concept of "charity." He was more than concerned for our welfare to the point of ultimate sacrifice; Jesus expressed an emotional love that could be felt. One cannot read the Gospel accounts and not be impressed with this fact. He wept for Lazarus. He wept for the multitudes. His dealings with the disciples were flavored with compassion and feeling and understanding. We must learn to love with that kind of love. Always remember this: *Love cannot exist without emotional content (affection).*

(6) *Basic desire for achievement.* This has reference to a sense of purpose and direction in life. Aimlessness, purposelessness, and lack of desire to achieve something in life are among the highest contributing causes to depression and suicidal tendencies. Basic to this level of responsibility is an understanding of the "spiritual gifts." A firm belief that God has given one special ability to accomplish a concrete objective is an enormous impetus in giving a man or woman a sense of purpose and direction.

(7) *Basic harmony of divine and human will.* The conflict in the mind of many believers about whether or not they are "in the will of God" must be dispelled if a balanced, effective Christian experience is to be achieved. The believer must be confident that he has the mind of Christ. He must learn not to emphasize his will as separate and distinct from God's will.

These *levels of responsibility* are essential to the healthy Christian personality. To the degree that they are achieved, to that degree the believer conforms to a consistent, well-ordered process of becoming like the perfect Christ. Bringing someone through each of these levels, beginning at the first and ending with the last, is the objective of the loving paracaletic therapist. Whether that person has a neurosis, psychosis, or personality disorder is of no consequence. The objectives and levels are the same. Obviously with some the process will be more complex and prolonged than others. But it is still the same process.

5

CONTRIBUTIONS OF EMINENT THEORISTS

The intent of this chapter is not to present and analyze the complex theories of men who by and large have formed the basic foundations of psychology today. Such a task would be incredibly huge, as Ellenberger's *Discovery of the Unconscious* bears witness. Such an analysis would be foreign to our purpose. We are interested, however, in certain tenets and methodologies of therapy that these men held, i.e., where they touch upon biblical principles.

SIGMUND FREUD

That Sigmund Freud was not a friend of Christianity is well documented. However, if we are broad-minded enough to admit that much of what he said was true (even about religion), we will discover that Freud was more of a religionist than he cared to admit. Still, that is not important to this study. What is important

is the answer to the question: Did Freud offer something worthwhile in the treatment of human problems as viewed in a Christian
context?

Psychoanalysis

I suppose it is too much to expect for some to believe that
Freud's mechanism of psychoanalysis is a valid technique in the
treatment of Christians with problems, or treatment of anyone for
that matter. I am convinced, however, that the psychoanalytic
method in the diagnosis of human behavior is a valid one. Not only
that, it is strongly implied if not directly indicated in Scripture. But
before we investigate scriptural validation, let us try to determine
the nature and function of psychoanalysis:

> In psychoanalytic technique the patient reclines on a
> couch, and the therapist sits on a chair behind him, seeing
> but unseen. The analyst explains the basic rule, which is
> to tell anything that comes to mind. This rule is, of course,
> difficult to follow, and the patient has to overcome resis-
> tances, which in the best of cases would never completely
> disappear. After a few weeks, however, the patient learns
> to overcome his resistance, and even to take pleasure in
> talking at random. A gradual loosening of associations
> occurs, and instead of following one train of thought, the
> subject jumps from one idea to another. As the analysis
> proceeds, more and more memories of even more remote
> childhood events appear interspersed with memories of
> dreams and fantasies, and the patient begins to have a
> strangely distorted picture of the analyst. The analyst
> offers interpretations.[1]

The purpose of all this is primarily to discover the basic problem
of the patient as well as its nuances and severity. Much can be
uncovered in this way. It also has its therapeutic value in what is
often referred to as "ventilation." That is, it gives the patient the

---

1. Henri F. Ellenberger, *The Discovery of the Unconscious* (New York: Basic
Books, Incorporated, Publishers, 1970), pp. 521, 522.

opportunity to get everything off the proverbial chest, and relief results.

It is noted then, that psychoanalysis has two-fold value: (1) *It aids in diagnosis.* (2) It provides *an atmosphere for ventilation* which brings relief. The interpretations of the analyst at this point seem to me valueless. The therapeutic value lies not in his remarks, but in the patient's opportunity and ability to articulate. The skill in this whole approach, however, is not interpretation, but in the delicate nature of (a) *trust* on the part of the patient and (b) *involvement* on the part of the therapist. He seeks to gain the confidence of the patient and to understand him and his problem.

The concept of the unseen analyst speaking from the darkness, offering interpretations of motivation and behavior, is weird if not downright childish. Further, probing into the patient's background often does not contribute to understanding what is wrong with him now to the extent that it will provide him with *therapeutic* insight. More likely, it will provide the patient with an excuse or a crutch for his present behavior. For example, he must never be led to believe that his ill relationship with his father, while influencing present behavior, also excuses it. He is still responsible for his actions. He must never excuse his present actions on the basis of a bad childhood or because of the circumstances of his life or whatever. The task of the therapist is to help the patient to cope with life as it exists for him now, not to provide an excuse for aberrant behavior.

It amazes me that some cannot see the value or contribution that psychoanalysis makes in the curing of the soul. The object of lying down is to relax and to relieve tension. This in itself often brings symptomatic relief. A relaxed, tensionless state of mind is an excellent place for therapy to begin. It is the time when the mind is often the most constructive. The following Scriptures seem to indicate that such a state of mind is beneficial and spiritually therapeutic:

> . . . commune with your own heart upon your bed, and be still (*Psalm 4:4*).

> When I call thee to mind upon my bed and think on thee in the watches of the night, remembering how thou hast been my help and that I am safe in the shadow of thy

wings, then I humbly follow thee with all my heart, and thy right hand is my support (*Psalm 63:6–8 NEB*).

David reminds us that communing with our "hearts" (mind) upon our bed is a form of introspection that can provide insight into our problems. For him, it was the analysis of certain sins he wished to avoid. It apparently was helpful for him to recall how God had blessed him in the course of the experiences of his life. By focusing upon his reliance on the Lord, David could find strength of soul. Such a time was appropriate to express his emotions and the thoughts that burdened him about the external pressures (his enemies) of his life:

I am weary with my groaning; all the night make I my bed to swim; I water my couch with my tears. Mine eye is consumed because of grief; it waxeth old because of all mine enemies (*Psalm 6:6, 7*).

The therapeutic effect of the experience is obvious:

The Lord will strengthen him upon the bed of languishing ... *heal my soul;* for I have sinned against thee (*Psalm 41:3, 4*).

Even Job, who had more reason for psychoses than most of us, said,

My bed shall comfort me, my couch shall ease my complaint ... (*Job 7:13*),

even though his friends would not give him the opportunity. (They were definitely not good therapists.)

I want to emphasize again, however, that such a concept of psychoanalysis is definitely to be substituted for that of the Freudian school. I see it as a tool for discovery, relief, and involvement. It must be further realized that psychoanalysis is not for everyone. Since not all patients will respond to this approach to their problem, other avenues must be explored in the search for a point of entry.

Dream Interpretation

A second beneficial and informative source for psychological insight is the patient's dreams. Again, and to a more limited extent, we are indebted to Freud for his work in this area. Perhaps I should say, we are most indebted to him for calling to our remembrance the importance of dreams and dream structure and content. I do not accept for a moment Freud's approach to the interpretation of dreams. It is nonetheless a fact that dreams often provide a rich source of information about the roots and bases of aberrant behavior.

Operating on the basis that the mind is a magnificent computer and recorder, we conclude that everything that the senses respond to, from the point in which they have capacity to respond, is recorded indelibly upon the mind. Proceeding on this theory, the mind can forget nothing. Everything that the five senses have fed into it has been placed in "memory cells," to be recalled upon proper stimuli. Some people have the ability to recall many scenes that occurred during infancy, scenes that for some esoteric or long-forgotten reason were important to them at the time.

By far, the vast portion of what our senses have been exposed to is no longer in our conscious mind. Actually, our conscious mind is simply whatever measure of awareness is occurring at any given moment. When we recall, we are simply varying our "awareness." Still, most of the experiences of life cannot be recalled at the whim of will. A very great amount can be recalled with strict, rigid, and structured mental force. But many things our senses record, like the noise on the freeway or the color of a building, go unnoticed. The vast amount of sensory exposure is not in our conscious, i.e., in our realm of awareness. We still recall these things sometimes at the most spontaneous and unlikely moments. Where have they been hidden? What stimulated their recall? Thus we give rise to the consideration of a mind within us that is not conscious but still real. We call it the unconscious. The conscious compared with the unconscious is like the tip of an iceberg. We are aware of that part of the ice which we can see. The part under the surface, which we can't see, is many times larger than what is exposed. Our conscious is only a fingernail compared to the huge body of the unconscious.

When we sleep, we achieve the ultimate relaxation of which our bodies are capable. The conscious mind is no longer operating to external stimuli. But the unconscious mind is not affected by the immediacy of sensory perception. The unconscious mind operates best when the conscious mind is in repose. Therefore, what has been recorded on the unconscious mind comes to the surface and forms dreams.

Things that affect the unconscious, or the *inner* man, in the most significant way usually spell out dream content. Therefore, dream content reveals the precise sensitivity of the inner person. What the inner person is most sensitive to is what the therapist is most interested in; the reason being that the unconscious often guides the conscious and therefore guides behavior. So it is helpful to know as much about the unconscious as possible. Dream content represents the things that may give rise to behavior.

Again, investigation into this area merely supplies the therapist with information about the patient. Such information better enables the therapist to diagnose what is wrong and the areas of irresponsibility upon which to concentrate. It is to be taken into consideration with all other sources of information, certainly not to be evaluated alone.

CARL GUSTAV JUNG

Jung was a Swiss psychiatrist who would perhaps enjoy more acceptance among Christian circles than Freud. Again, his theory is far too complex and lengthy to study here and is foreign to our purpose. But he made one discovery, or shall I say *rediscovery,* of something vital for the Christian counselor to bear in mind.

Pathogenic Secrets

It has been my experience to talk with many people in deep need of mental and spiritual help. Some have been severe. Consider the case of Charles:

I heard Charles before I saw him. I entered a sleazy hotel in downtown Anaheim, knowing only that a man there had called me for help. The clerk glared at me over her dirty wire-rimmed glasses and mumbled the number of the room. The elevator was no larger than 4 X 4 feet, and when the accordion-like cage door slammed shut and the dumbwaiter doors closed I felt somewhat trapped. The elevator doors opened at the third floor and I could hear a hacking cough that made me wonder if someone's whole insides were being expectorated on the floor. My apprehension increased when I discovered that the hacking came from behind the door upon which I knocked. Between coughs, I was able to discern, "Come in, the door's open." I entered and what I saw brought a wave of nausea. A man was sprawled on an unmade, disheveled bed, clothes soiled with vomit, a bearded stubble of a face, brown eyes that bulged enormously, and black matted hair. This was my first encounter with Charles.

His first words were apologies about not cleaning up and he thanked me for coming. His sentences were barely understandable because of his uncontrollable coughing. Finally, it subsided enough for him to begin to tell his story. It came in bits and pieces, sometimes incoherent, sometimes coherent, interspersed with fits of coughing. He shook as he had to spit several times. He never seemed to get it all out and he ended up wiping his mouth with the tail of his shirt.

His story revealed that Charles was not always like this. He was once a certified public accountant. At one time he owned his own business. He was a lecturer in the humanities and in business procedure. As all of this came out, I was appalled that this could be the same man: the responsible citizen he once was. His main problem now, according to him, was that he wanted to go back home to his family, but his wife would not have him. His daughters loved him, he said, but his wife was implacable.

Obviously I was getting only the picture that Charles wanted me to see, so I began probing. Why did his wife want nothing to do with him? He didn't know. He supposed it was because she felt that he drank too much. Did he drink too much? No, of course not. This was the way it went, one obvious question after another. His answers indicated that he really couldn't see why he lost his job, why his wife wouldn't have him, etc. Then he made a passing remark about his first wife having the same trouble.

The interview continued this way until I left. I had about five sessions with Charles, each one more frustrating than the one before. I talked with his wife and family, and she was determined that he would never darken her door again. In one session with him, I recalled the reference he made about his first wife and asked how things had been with her. I asked whether she had married again, simply trying to get him to talk about it. He became very evasive and began to mumble something about its being all his fault, that he was no good, and on and on. I interjected from time to time that he was important to God and that the Lord wanted to help him now. The reference to God's benevolence seemed to make him worse. He said that God couldn't care about him, that God had rejected him, that he was too bad, that he had done something unforgivable. Here it came out.

I had stumbled upon what Jung calls a pathogenic secret. In uncontrollable sobs Charles told me that he had killed his first wife. He had done it with a knife. He had been tried and acquitted, but he knew that he had murdered her. This is why he had never had a decent job in the five years since it had happened. This is why he drank so much. This is why he was such a miserable wreck. This is why he felt so completely dependent upon his present wife.

Charles, in the emotion of the moment, made a profession of faith in Christ. His wife, I discovered, was also a Christian. But she seemed to be one of these fire-breathing fundamentalists who had as much love for Charles as she would for a dog with mange. However, in the name of "Christian grace," she would at my recommendation try to live with Charles once again. She tried. The next day Charles was back in the hotel. Her story: in the middle of the night while the family was asleep, leaving her husband comfortably watching television, she awoke to find Charles standing over her with a raised butcher knife in his hand.

Incredible, you say? Was Charles a homicidal psychopath? I don't know. Shortly after that, Charles lost interest in my efforts to help him. He apparently thought that I hadn't succeeded and he wouldn't respond to me any more. I tried reaching him at the hotel and couldn't. The last I heard, he was in touch with another minister.

The point of this lurid tale is that people often have experiences that leave their mark on them for life. If Charles was telling me the truth, he had murdered his first wife and had gotten away with it. And if his second wife was telling me the truth, he wasn't above trying it again. These pathogenic secrets often are the root of aberrant behavior. The Christian therapist must concentrate his therapy on this point of entry in the first steps of involvement.

CARL ROGERS

Rogers is not in the same monumental league with Freud and Jung, but he has introduced to psychotherapy a basically sound technique. What he has done with it and what others have done with it are another matter.

Client-Centered Therapy

Rogers pointed out that counseling consists of a definitely structured, permissive relationship which allows the client to gain an understanding of himself to a degree that enables him to take positive steps in the light of his new orientation.[2] Put more simply, the therapist helps the client to help himself. Rogers' methodology of arriving at that goal, while sometimes workable, is in my opinion inadequate.

Using this technique, the counselor refrains from telling the counselee the nature of his problem or anything like what he should do about it. The whole program of the therapist is to keep the patient talking. A very brief example of this approach might be:

> *Patient:* Doctor, my life is falling apart. I can't concentrate. I can't make friends with people I work with. I am antagonistic. Everything is wrong and I am miserable.

> *Doctor:* You mean that your life is sort of falling apart at the seams, is that it?

> *Patient:* Yes. I can't seem to relate to other people and I always catch them whispering about me.

> *Doctor:* And how do you feel about that?

> *Patient:* Well, I get angry. How would you feel?

> *Doctor:* Then what happens?

2. Carl Rogers, *Counseling and Psychotherapy: Newer Concepts in Practice* (Boston: Houghton Mifflin Company, 1942).

On it goes. The counselor continues to prompt and never advises, but hopes in his one-sided conversations that the patient will slowly begin to understand the corrective measures necessary to cure him. This is not so far-fetched as it may sound. The fact is, most people realize that what they are doing is out of joint with normalcy, and to articulate it is to objectify it. Such objectivity is decidedly therapeutic. Still, Rogers' methodology has a number of serious problems which without modification are unacceptable to Christian therapy.

(1) *It does not recognize that man does not have the resources within himself to cure a spiritual ill.* This is not to deny that a lot of non-Christian, well-adjusted people are running around. But it does suggest that anyone who does have incapacitating problems will not find the solution to his problem in his incapacity. There must be a responsible norm against which he can measure himself and from which he can draw guidance.

(2) *It does not recognize the capacity of the Holy Spirit operating through the life of another believer, i.e., the counselor.* One might argue that the Holy Spirit is in the counselee too, if he is a Christian. And he would be right. So why not shut the counselee up with a Bible and tell him to work it out on his own? Unfortunately, this has been the approach of many Christian counselors. It is terribly easy for one familiar with the promises of the Bible simply to parrot them, or write references down on paper and pass them on to the counselee in the form of spiritual aspirin. Or, one might say that because the Holy Spirit is in the counselee, then Rogers's technique is valid because the Holy Spirit will ultimately guide him to find the right answer. This is true. It can and often does happen. The simple association with another person who parrots his words back to him would then act as a mirror and help him to see with the Spirit's help exactly what needs to be healed.

But while this does happen at times, the counselor must realize that the counselee came to *him* for help. And the counselor must realize that the Spirit of God broadly and continuously uses men to minister his services to men. This is the beauty of Paul's statement:

> For I long to see you, that I may impart unto you some
> spiritual gift, to the end ye may be established; That is,

that I may be comforted [from *paracaleo*] together with you by the mutual faith both of you and me (*Romans 1:11, 12*).

It is unfortunate that Christians, in their zeal either to defend the faith (which is more often their system of doctrine) or to resist the non-Christian tenets of Freud, Jung, or Rogers, have "thrown out the baby with the bathwater." These men have made an enormous contribution to the science of understanding the *homo sapiens* mentality. They view their findings through the eyes of humanism, but aren't we the losers if we fail to appreciate truth regardless of its apparent source?

6

DIAGNOSIS

Dr. Richard M. Hawes of the Institute for Reality Therapy has clearly indicated that diagnosis does not play a significant role in Reality Therapy. Except for this one feature, Reality Therapy is still the point of view that I feel is most valid in the treatment of psychiatric patients.

It seems to me that if I am to help another, I must know where he hurts. I must know as much about the person and his problem as I possibly can, within the context of my association with him. This is the function of diagnosis: *To know, and to evaluate and treat in the light of that knowledge.* A statement that one professor made in a class long ago has stuck with me through the years. He said, "There are two things a competent counselor must know to help people. He must *know the man* and he must *know the message."* The man is the patient, and the message is the truth that will help him. While this may be oversimplified, it is basically true. I am always amazed how a doctor can know how to prescribe medicine from memory. He examines, formulates a diagnosis, and prescribes. The Christian therapist should be equally adept in his knowledge of the patient and what it takes to help him.

This is the biggest flaw in current psychological treatments. Psychologists and the like make marvelously detailed diagnoses. They are generally right, but they don't have the right "medicine chest." Or shall I say, they go to the wrong source. True, they know by experimentation which treatment is best suited for a specific problem. But, forgive the analogy, it's a bit like the witch doctor knowing which herb to use and which rattle to shake—if the therapist ignores God. Even Christian psychologists who are not trained in the Scriptures, or are only meagerly trained, will ordinarily depend too much on their knowledge of the man.

Ministers, on the other hand, often don't deal with the real problem. They are often too rushed with other things to discover what it is and consequently they deal only with symptoms. Many don't understand or even care about the unconscious, i.e., the inner person and his conflicts. Someone in trouble may come to them desiring a one-to-one relationship with a counselor, with God, with somebody; and all too often that person is simply given advice or a "life verse," is prayed over, and sent on his way. These "men of the cloth" may be well versed in the Scriptures, but they don't understand the man—nor do they want to. They are too busy being the chief executive of their own little bailiwick. They are working their respective heads off trying to build one of the great churches of America. Perhaps they love their job too much to be concerned about the people who need them.

While it may or may not be a good place to start, it simply isn't enough to ask a man or woman "what's wrong." The patient may not be able to articulate it coherently. This is why involvement, *loving involvement,* is so critical.

PSYCHOANALYSIS

Perhaps, in order to be fair to Freud and those physicians who practice Freudian psychoanalysis, we should not refer to our suggestions along this line as "psychoanalysis." What we are suggesting certainly is not Freudian psychoanalysis. But we do feel that at least an adaptation of the Freudian technique is extremely valuable in correct diagnosis. Remember the purpose of this method, spoken of previously: Involvement with the patient, understanding his problem, and giving him the opportunity to "get everything off his chest."

Some means should be available for the subject to lie down and he should be encouraged to relax completely. He should then be instructed to say whatever comes to his mind. He will feel awkward at first, but eventually he will become eased. The therapist should prompt the subject with certain key questions which may or may not have direct bearing on the reason why the subject came to him. A sense of companionship should be achieved.

Actually, this procedure simply adds another dimension to what otherwise might be called an interview. That dimension is an atmosphere of comfort and relaxation. Notes should be taken by the therapist about the emotional climate of the counselee and on salient points of his narrative which bear further investigation. These points may be significant experiences he has had, emotional expression such as hostility evidenced while relating something, weeping, reticence to discuss something, evasion, and the like. Expertise in recognizing significant things the counselee says can come only with experience. After a session such as this, the counselee will often "feel better." This is good. The therapist can be assured that the session was at least partly constructive. These sessions may continue as long as the therapist concludes that they are helping the patient, or until he feels he has the information on which to build a sound therapeutic approach.

The question will undoubtedly surface as to how much time should be spent in this sort of thing. The first guideline one may follow is to remember the primary function of the procedure: diagnosis. As soon as the therapist feels that he has a thorough grasp of the problem, he may discontinue this approach. It may be after only one session, or it may take several. Don't be in too big a rush, but don't waste time either.

One of the biggest minuses, in my opinion, is the long duration of therapeutic sessions that most therapists follow when employing traditional methodology. I believe that progress should be made from the very first encounter with a patient. It has been my experience that prolonged counseling is often unnecessary. Many therapists think in terms of a year or more. I prefer to think in terms of months or even weeks. The rapidity of therapeutic process depends, in our work, upon the time it takes to gain involvement. From that point on, things should move rapidly.

THE INTERVIEW

An immense amount of information is made available through simple conversation. The first objective in an interview is the elimination of pretense. One psychologist I know does not even display his degrees where the patient can see them. He feels as though their presence constitutes a "put down" for the counselee. I tend to agree, although some patients doubtless have their confidence in the competence of the therapist bolstered when they see evidence of his academic achievements. One of the objectives of involvement is to be a friend to the patient, not a distant professional clinician.

In the Christian perspective, the counselee should be made to feel that a relationship of love exists between him and the therapist. He should feel that the therapist sincerely wants to help him. The reason he should "feel" it is because the therapist *should* feel love for him and do what he can to communicate it. If the patient is to have complete confidence, he must feel that the therapist has only his welfare at heart. Then he will unload voluntarily and will withhold very little.

TESTING

Certain psychological tests can be of value in understanding what makes the counselee function as he does. However, unless the minister is licensed by his state, it is unlawful for him to use these tests (he cannot even obtain them through normal channels).

Some tests are available to him, which provide excellent insight into the problems of the one needing help. One such psychological test is *The Luscher Color Test,* prepared by Dr. Max Luscher, which can be purchased at any bookstore and most newsstands. It has been printed in paperback by Pocket Books, New York, and was originally published by Random House, Inc. I have used this test on myself and many others. I have a great deal of confidence in it and have found it helpful in my counseling ministry.

The following is a battery of questions that have been helpful in discovering the "type" of person a prospective counselee might be, along with insight into potential problem areas. The responses to the questions are either: *Yes* or *No*. Analysis of the responses will indicate personality strength as well as those areas that need therapeutic attention. Many of the questions are similar. The frequency and nature of responses to a certain question type may be significant.

1. Do you always plan ahead?
2. Do you smoke?
3. Do you like to drive?
4. Is Jesus God?
5. Do you feel that "the cards are always stacked against you?"
6. Are you always in a hurry?
7. Do you have a strong sex drive?
8. Are your thoughts often confused and jumbled?
9. Does taking a test like this irritate you?
10. Are you very lonely?
11. Do you like to wear expensive clothes?
12. Do you often refuse when someone asks you to do something?
13. Do you change your mind easily?
14. Do you consider yourself a warm, personable person?
15. Are you frightened about the results of this test?
16. Can you recall at least three major successes in your life?
17. Does long hair on men offend you?
18. Do you like the police?
19. Do you have positive goals in life?
20. Would you continue pursuit of an objective to the hurt of others?
21. Do you smoke heavily?
22. Do you believe in God?
23. Do people behind you worry you when driving?
24. Is Jesus your Savior?
25. Do you get angry when people "talk down" to you?
26. Is the world a beautiful place?
27. Do you daydream about the opposite sex?

28. Do you take daily naps?
29. Do you like to travel?
30. Do people mistreat you?
31. Do you groom yourself meticulously?
32. Do you take orders easily?
33. Are you easily influenced?
34. Do you give to charitable organizations?
35. Are you afraid in the dark?
36. Do you diet often?
37. Do you feel unsafe in an airplane?
38. Are you a pacifist?
39. Do you have definite lifetime goals?
40. Does Jesus speak to you audibly?
41. Do you believe people are talking about you?
42. Do loud noises startle you?
43. Do you like to "make your point"?
44. Is Jesus your Lord?
45. Do you feel sorry for people who are incompetent?
46. Do you enjoy picking flowers?
47. Do you consider yourself a sensual person?
48. Do you sleep well?
49. Do you like being with others your age?
50. Are you an active person?
51. Do you brush your teeth more than once a day?
52. Do you love someone of the same sex very much?
53. Do you influence others positively?
54. Do you eat everything on your plate?
55. Do you think that you would die for your country?
56. Do you have a weight problem?
57. Do you feel closed in?
58. Do you avoid discussing certain subjects?
59. Does your life revolve around others?
60. Do you fear the unseen world?
61. Do you embarrass easily?
62. Are most of your dreams pleasant?
63. Do you consider yourself a fool?
64. Do you attend church?
65. Do you feel that you have an equal opportunity in the world?

66. Do you enjoy being around the boys?
67. Do you approve of premarital intercourse?
68. Are you an early riser?
69. Are you a loner?
70. Do you participate in any physical sports?
71. Do you bathe or shower once a day?
72. Do you love someone of the opposite sex very much?
73. Do you have a savings account?
74. Do aggressive people annoy you?
75. Are you a "right winger"?
76. Do you have trouble keeping a job?
77. Do you have many allergies?
78. Is Jesus a real living person to you?
79. Do you feel that you must put your children through college?
80. Do you believe in ghosts?
81. Do you have a pet peeve?
82. Do you worry about what your dreams may mean?
83. Do you prefer others to take the responsibility?
84. Do you read the Bible regularly?
85. Do circumstances upset you?
86. Do you enjoy being around girls?
87. Do you consider masturbation harmful?
88. Do you see a bright future for yourself?
89. Do you consider yourself a maverick?
90. Are you a chess player?
91. Do you put on a fresh change of underwear each day?
92. Do you feel love for your parents?
93. Are you making payments on indebtedness?
94. Are you generally an aggressive person?
95. Are you in sympathy with anti-communist movements?
96. Do you change jobs often?
97. Do you see your doctor often?
98. Do you enjoy a good fight?
99. Have you ever failed drastically?
100. Is good luck your companion?
101. Do loud and boistrous people annoy you?
102. Do you enjoy being successful?
103. Do you have any hobbies?

104. Do you have a favorite sport?
105. Do you enjoy being the center of attraction?
106. Do you have trouble remembering?
107. Do you budget your money?
108. Do you have a strong sense of right and wrong?
109. Are you significantly overweight?
110. Do you usually go along with the crowd?
111. Would you like for Christ to control your life?
112. Will you take a chance?
113. Do you enjoy a good movie?
114. Do you love God?
115. Do you have life insurance?
116. Are you a "peacemaker"?
117. Do you enjoy hunting?
118. Do you feel guilty often?
119. Are you in good general health?
120. Is the opinion of others very important to you?
121. Do you ever think about taking your own life?
122. Have you ever been to a seance?
123. Do you make friends easily?
124. Do you like to be one who leads others?
124. Do you consider yourself on an equal plane with others?
126. Do you have any close friends?
127. Is seeing the "bright side" of things difficult for you?
128. Do you consider money very important?
129. Are you right most of the time?
130. Do you enjoy eating?
131. Will you stand up against an obvious majority if you feel you are right?
132. Does any form of gambling appeal to you?
133. Do you watch television more than 20 hours a week?
134. Do you love everybody?
135. Do you have health insurance?
136. Are you shy and retiring?
137. Are you heavily in debt?
138. Does "rock music" annoy you?
139. Are you sick often?
140. Do you care what other people think?
141. Do other people like you?

142. Do you pray often?
143. Are you an outdoors type person?
144. Do you consider yourself a follower?
145. Are you annoyed with incompetence?
146. Are you afraid for others to know your faults?
147. Do you love animals?
148. Do you read novels, biographies, nonfiction?
149. Do you weigh each decision carefully?
150. Do you like to eat out?
151. Do you usually seek the point of least resistance?
152. Are you willing to risk everything for a worthwhile goal?
153. Do you like to pretend you are someone else?
154. Do you make a lot of mistakes?
155. Does the sight of blood affect you badly?
156. Do you have many friends?
157. Do you often feel you can't measure up?
158. Do you drink alcoholic beverages often?
159. Are speed limits always important to you?
160. Do you enjoy quiet evenings at home?
161. Do children like you?
162. Were you at fault in more than two auto accidents?
163. Are you ever sexually attracted to people of the same sex?
164. Do heights make you feel uneasy?
165. Are you an initiator?
166. Do you lose your temper often?
167. Are you afraid of anybody?
168. Do you love children?
169. Do you read the editorial page of the newspaper?
170. Do you make quick decisions?
171. Would you like to see an "X" rated movie?
172. Do you feel that a person who does not work should not eat?
173. Do you own stock?
174. Is someone your idol?
175. Do you enjoy opera?
176. Do you chase fire trucks often?
177. Are you generally satisfied with life?
178. Do you often do things "just for the ducks of it"?

179. Do you "second gear stop" stop signs often?
180. Is housework drudgery for you?
181. Are you an avid reader?
182. Do animals like you?
183. Do you enjoy sex?
184. Are you a meticulous, organized person?
185. Are you a responder?
186. Do you cry easily?
187. Do you feel that some people plot against you?
188. Do older people annoy you?
189. Do you read "advice" columns?
190. Are you a well-organized person?
191. Do you read *Playboy* magazine or the equivalent?
192. Do you enjoy being alone?
193. Do you drive a large car?
194. Do you admire and respect someone very much?
195. Do you find certain music relaxing?
196. Do you act because you are afraid of the consequences if you do not?
197. Are you a happy, well-adjusted person?
198. Do you fear failure?
199. Do others let you down often?
200. Are you totally committed to some objective?

These questions are designed to probe into the values and feelings of the patient. Hopefully he will be honest in his answers; he should be encouraged to be. But he will not be honest if he thinks the therapist will form judgmental opinions of him. This is why loving involvement which produces mutual trust is so important. The answers to the above questions will provide knowledge about the counselee's self-image, egocentricity, hostility, depression, suicidal tendency, mores, motivation, compassion, fears, and anxieties. This kind of information is invaluable when preparing therapeutic technique.[1]

However good testing may be for diagnostic use, nothing is so completely satisfying in our understanding of an individual as

1. The test itself and the kit necessary for proper interpretation may be ordered from Neighborhood Family Services, Box 5206, Garden Grove, California 92645.

involvement in a love relationship. Jesus knew how to communicate: he could communicate with the masses, with a few individuals, or with just one. But the keynote of his communication with people was his compassion and love for them. The omniscient factor of Christ's knowledge while he was incarnate was severely limited—limited, in fact, to the knowledge that the Father revealed to him on specific occasions. Jesus had to rely by and large on his own interaction and interrelationships to make his love felt. Through the Person of the Holy Spirit, he is active in the continued communication of that love through believers today.

SYMPTOMATIC SIGNALS

When you read what follows you may wonder why I didn't refer to these problems as basic maladies instead of symptoms. I realize that many psychologists and even Christian psychologists may scoff at the idea that any human problem that is not physiological is of necessity spiritual. I use spiritual here in the sense of whatever forms the immaterial part of man, lumping the soul and the spirit together. In fact, I don't consider it presumptuous to suggest that even physiological problems involve spiritual and mental considerations. Suggesting that a malady is a "spiritual problem" is simply another way of saying that what we see in the behavior pattern of an individual represents in some measure a deeper departure from a well-balanced relationship with God. This is not to suggest that illnesses are always the result of sin. I am saying that something is out of spiritual adjustment and needs to be brought back into focus.

I resist the idea that every irregularity in behavior is always the consequence of some mysterious sin that a believer may be harboring. Such an approach to Christian aberrant behavior reflects more on the accusative nature of the therapist than it casts light on a counselee's problem. But this does not influence the fact that the "apparent" problem has a deeper root in the spirit and psyche of the patient. He must be helped to view his difficulty as something in which God can have a hand. Only the symptoms which I feel are the most pressing and widespread among believers are listed

below. Somehow, it seems that God's people are not exempt from
any mental irregularity that plagues people, but these are the ones
most frequent in my experience.

Depression

A depressed person is someone who has an unreasonable view
of his own lack of worth. He feels rejected, unloved, inadequate,
and worthless. He sees no optimistic future for himself and often
determines that he has no reason to live. He has concluded that he
is no good to anyone and can make little if any contribution to life.
This is a very dismal, miserable person who is desperately in need
of help.

Causes for depression, for the most part, center around hostility
turned inward. The subject is upset with himself and cannot
accept himself for what he is—with his faults and with his positive attributes. He sees only his faults. Depression may be the
result of some terrible experience that he has not yet adjusted to
a balanced personality. (Psychology refers to this as Reactive
Depression. I may as well state here what the reader will undoubtedly notice, that psychological categories and terms are studiously
avoided. In my opinion they serve to clarify little, and the danger
of "labeling" and boxing in a client with these terms is often prohibitive to adequate involvement. *It is not necessary to use these
terms.* A number of psychologists, with whom I discussed this
matter at length, state flatly that they no longer considered these
technical terms important and that they used them only
rarely.)

A depressed person's strong sense of guilt is often caused
by parental neglect or maltreatment when a child. This insight may not provide a great deal of therapeutic help, but a depressed person's present condition may be and often is linked
directly to the manner of early life. If a child was constantly
threatened by a parent, or if the parent failed to meet the child's
need for love, and if the child was made to feel unwanted and unloved, the resulting depression in adult life is almost inevitable.

In most books of this nature, a procedure for treatment is usually
sketched after certain symptoms are described. I have chosen to

withhold my remarks about treatment until a later chapter on therapeutic techniques.

Psychoses and Neuroses

A distinction should be made between basic phenomena that occur in aberrant human behavior. At the risk of being simplistic, let me simply state that neuroses are generally associated with anxiety, tension, and disorders of the central nervous system. Generally speaking, neuroses occur in a somewhat milder form than psychoses, or shall I say are less a menace to society and the individual. However, this does not always hold true. It certainly is not uncommon for a neurotic person to be institutionalized. But the frequency of hospitalization is higher with the psychotic.

Psychoses generally are evident by thought disorder. Hallucinations, absurd and unreasonable thoughts and actions accompany the psychotic. If a person has concluded that he has grown a three-foot furry tail, he has encountered a thought disorder and is said to be psychotic.

This is not an attempt to be funny about a serious malady, but someone has remarked that a psychotic adds two plus two and gets five. A neurotic adds two plus two and gets four, but is unhappy about it. The study of these two fields is important to anyone who will take counseling seriously. The reader is encouraged to consult the bibliography for references to works which will be helpful in his understanding of psychoses and neuroses.

Problems with Morality

This again is a very common problem for Christian people especially. The reason believers seem to have such a problem is because of repression of the sexual drive in view of what they consider unacceptable sexual behavior. In our opinion, the Christian world of today has overstepped the scriptural teachings about the control of sexual feelings. Evangelical Christianity is incredibly inconsistent with regard to general scriptural "prohibitions." Ministers raise a furor about mini-skirts, but permit their daughters and wives to wear abbreviated swimsuits on the beach and in pools—indeed, they themselves go along and enjoy the scenery. Thunders of condemnation about the evils of smoking can be heard in count-less evangelical churches—from obese ministers of the gospel. Children are told to "obey your parents," while mom and dad fight and squabble, exceed speed limits, and run stop signs. Movies are hailed as being from the pit of hell—and after his sermon the preacher goes home to watch Raquel Welch on TV.

Frankly, it is my feeling that most of the Bible "prohibitions" do not find their source in Scripture at all, but in medieval theology. The two aren't necessarily the same. If believers were more realistic about life and its demands, and would trust the Spirit who is in them to "lead them in the paths of righteousness for his namesake," they would be a lot happier and well adjusted. In short, it is my conviction that most Christian moral problems are not "problems" at all from the scriptural viewpoint. Granted, it most certainly is a problem to the person who considers it such; and likely, the best therapy is to give him a proper understanding of what the Scripture really does teach about the matter. But here are some sexual abuses about which Scripture is quite definitive:

Adultery

Adultery is a technical term relating only to married people. *It is the violation of the love commitment between two people.* The unifying sub-stratum of marriage is a commitment, not "vows" parroted at a rather artificial and euphoric wedding ceremony. When one commits adultery the partner is hurt. The blame for this hurt is to be laid at the feet of the offending partner. When he has hurt the one to whom he has committed himself, he has violated his commitment of love. Whatever love does, it never seeks the damage of another.

Fornication

Fornication is a much broader term in Scripture than adultery. Its primary meaning includes all forms of immorality, and that is how it is translated in the more accurate translations. It includes incest, prostitution, and homosexuality.

Homosexuality

The homosexual is probably the most difficult subject for the Christian counselor to treat. Involvement with such a person is a repugnant idea to those who are not homosexuals. We should remember that involvement does not mean acceptance of aberrant behavior. It does mean acceptance of the individual for his intrinsic worth to God and society and to the therapist himself.

Can a Christian be a practicing homosexual? That the homosexual act is a sin is not a debatable question. The Bible is clear and abundant in its condemnation of it. Also, the Scripture is plain in its position that a Christian cannot *practice* sin. However, these two facts don't answer all the questions about this matter. Nor do they tell us how to view the person who professes to know and love Jesus Christ, yet cannot restrain himself from sinning in this manner.

First, it is necessary to divorce from the concept of homosexuality that it is somehow unique among sins. Sin, however it demonstrates itself, is still nothing more or less than sin. Perhaps the question should be, "Can a Christian be a practicing sinner?" Some people would erroneously view this question differently from the first (can a Christian be a practicing homosexual?). James points out that if anyone sins in only one point, "then he is guilty of all" (presumably the moral Law of God).

The matter focuses, then, upon a firm idea of what is meant by "practicing" sin. We cannot deny that whether saved or lost a person is nonetheless a sinner. All Christians are still sinners and continue throughout their lives to commit sin. Is this practicing sin? I don't know of any biblical scholar who would admit that. Some contend that this has reference to *habitual* sin. Again, there are particular sins that all of us habitually commit (running stop signs, eating too much, not loving our brother, etc.).

The only way to harmonize the two concepts that a Christian cannot practice sin, and yet in an undeniable sense, he does sin anyway, is to dig deeper into the matters of motivation and subsequent guilt. It cannot be true that a regenerated man can ignore completely the presence of the Holy Spirit in his life. For example, he cannot deliberately with malice and highhandedness enjoy plotting against God. It must be remembered that a Christian is a "son" of God, and that his "seed" remains in him, and he cannot sin (in this way) because he is born of God. One of the ministries of the Holy Spirit's presence is to bring conviction, which he does admirably.

It may be said therefore that a Christian (a) will find it impossible to commit sin without definite knowledge that he is doing wrong, and (b) will subsequently regret it because he has saddened his heavenly Father. Because of weakness, he may repeat it again and again. *But, however gradually, he will grow spiritually and will stop sinning in that way.* It is in his nature to do this. Through the agency of the Holy Spirit operating within the believer, or by association with the Word or perhaps a Christian counselor, he cannot do anything but do this. It is like the healing of a sore. It may take a long time, but it will heal. A Christian, then, can commit sin—frequently. This sin may be the homosexual act. But as certain as the sun rises, he will feel guilty about it, and in time will mature out of it.

Suicide

What causes people to want to commit suicide? According to some authorities, it occurs most often when someone is on his way into acute depression or possibly out of it. Whatever the cause behind suicide, the threat of it must be taken seriously. While it is true that some people will threaten suicide in order to get their way and manipulate others, such a threat must never be dismissed as insincere unless there is clear and abundant reason for doing so. Even then, be careful.

How can a potential suicide be recognized? Here are some signs to look for:

(1) Sudden, acute depression.
(2) Chronic, long-term depression.
(3) Loss of weight and appetite.
(4) Expressed desire to commit suicide.
(5) Chronic inability to sleep, nightmares, fear of sleep.
(6) Consistent, compulsive thoughts of suicide.
(7) Inability to express hostility directly.
(8) Directing of hostility back upon themselves.
(9) Overwhelming, incapacitating guilt feelings.
(10) Poor relationships with others and minimal relationship with God.

It is imperative to remember that a real potential suicide is a matter of which the authorities should be informed. If someone actually takes his own life and another knew that he might, that other person may be held indirectly responsible if he fails to notify the authorities.

There are many symptomatic expressions of aberrant behavior, but I shall evade the temptation to discuss them. There are many fine reference works in print which are available to the Christian counselor. Areas of specific and important study are husband-wife, parent-teenager, and parent-child relationships. Please consult the references at the end of this volume.

PART III

Restructuring the Christian Mind

7

A CHALLENGE
TO LEGALISM

No one will argue the point that a Christian must grow individually. Is it possible that the Church at large, the Body of Christ, can grow spiritually in a similar fashion? Most individual Christians when they are spiritually immature are rather didactic in their beliefs and often intolerant. But when they mature, they mellow somewhat and tend to become more understanding, more loving, more tolerant. They gain in their knowledge of "the message and the man."

I feel that the same should be true for the Church. Many "tenets of faith," in particular those governing Christian conduct and behavior, have untenable scriptural foundation. The problem exists today much like the problem that existed in the Galatian church. Paul dealt harshly and stringently with them for their penchant toward codification of Christian conduct.

In almost all evangelical circles, a structure of legalism has been erected. It is not unlike the wall of more than 600 human commandments built by the old rabbis around the Mosaic Law. When

3

Constantine institutionalized the church, it provided a womb for the birth of "church authority." With this authority came a whole new system of law, Christian law. During the Middle Ages when the institutionalized church wielded incredible political and psychological power, freedom and liberty in Christ were virtually mesmerized. Out of this black background grew the Reformation and still later, Puritanism. While the puritans gave us many rich inheritances, they also left us a legacy of cold, formalistic, non-involved religion. Even today, our theological mentality is strongly flavored by it.

The purpose of Part III is to challenge these influences. I don't claim to be an Apostle Paul writing to correct wrong attitudes and legalistic practices in the Galatian church, but I earnestly recommend that we Christians reexamine our way of living in the light of freedom and grace as set forth in Scripture.

SELF-PORTRAIT

I have wide and varied interests, a fact that has been a source of excitement to me as well as a source of failure and frustration. I have wanted to be a policeman, an armed forces chaplain, a professional athlete, to name just a few. I have many hobbies. I like to work in the yard, play handball, tennis, and golf. I teach swimming and lifesaving, scuba diving, etc. This is just *me*. I thoroughly enjoy the countless challenges and pleasures of life. I don't hesitate to say that I live life to the fullest.

At one point in my Christian life I made the foolish statement that I would never be the pastor of a church. I had been well acquainted with the awesome problems of church relationships, political maneuvering, and frustrated projects and programs. I had no inclination to be a hand-holder to a "bunch of Christian neurotics"! I had certainly soured on anything that resembled a pastoral ministry. I wanted no truck with people, their stubbornness, and their problems.

But when the opportunity came along I took it. I have been in it ever since. Much in the ministry today will discourage prospective ministers. I want to emphasize, however, that it is sublimely worth any struggle, any sacrifice. I have made many mistakes in my pastoral ministry. I have brought most of my unpleasant experiences upon myself (as is the case with most ministers).

Now, I am deeply in love with my ministry. There is a magnificent reason for this. I am profoundly in love with people. I find immense joy and satisfaction in being involved in their problems —and their being involved in mine. I never want to do anything else but be with people and be God's representative as he grants me the power to influence individuals in his love.

8

CONCEPT OF GOD

One of the saddest things I have witnessed in my ministry is the terrible concept that the vast majority of Christians (whether ministers or laypersons) have of God. A few days ago I asked my six-year-old son to tell me what he thought God was like. "Well," he said, "I think he's a big strong man who wears pants! He lives in heaven far away and he looks down on us to see how good we are, and he smashes us if we don't be good!"

I was shaken. Where did he get an idea like that? Did he get this concept of God from me? Is this how he views me? Granted, he's felt the rap of my knuckles on his head, but I never—*I am just not like that!*—I think.

Wherever he got it, it's certain that God didn't give it to him. Yet this description is how most believers view God. He is considered retributive, hard to please, and always demanding impossible things to do. He is someone who is going to call us on the carpet. So most of us view him with dread. This concept of God the Father has caused almost irreparable harm to the Church in general and to countless individuals. If we Christians are communicating this kind of image of God we are helping no one. We are giving a *false* impression. We are wrong—horribly wrong. One of the first places to begin our efforts to "restructure" the Christian mind is with our concept of God.

If someone were to ask you what you thought God was like, what would you say? Although less directly and pungently than my six-year-old, you might just give a similar answer to this question. Perhaps you would begin with the holiness of God, and then discuss his justice, and then his wrath against sin, and then you might allude to the fact that this God of yours is after all, a God of love. I don't think very many people would like your God. You are giving a distorted description of him.

I think we must start with his identity. We must understand that he is first of all one God expressed in three personalities. This is the most beautiful example of the nature of the Church. We are all individual personalities, but we are *one* in the Spirit, we are *one* in the Lord. God is *one,* but we view him in three personalities: Father, Son, and Holy Spirit.

Father

It is certainly not my objective to rehash the obvious. We all know certain essential attributes that help identify God the Father to us by virtue of the fact that they belong only to him. Basically, we are concerned here with God's frame of mind toward each of us as individuals, though mere mortals. Therefore, in addition to his all-knowing, all-powerful, everywhere-present, eternal, unchangeable essence, God the Father is above all, a real live Person. John's Gospel tells us that his substance is not flesh and blood, but spirit. He has a personality of will, intellect, and emotion all his own. Moreover, it appears that his primary preoccupation, in addition to such matters as creation, etc., is with us humans, collectively and individually.

We must remember that we have been created in his image and likeness, and because of this we bear direct kinship with him. No other created being shares this kinship with us. Only man was created in the image of God.

This gives God a unique interest vested in us alone. Logic demands that this interest is benevolent. In other words, God's attitude toward us works to our benefit. We belong to him. He cannot help but want us to think of him positively. God wants us to know that he is our *Father*. We share his nature in some way enigmatically similar to our tie with our earthly fathers.

When Jesus told the Pharisees, "Ye are of your father the devil," he did not mean that they were created in Satan's image, or that they shared anything with Satan that was not a matter of choice. However, we do not choose to be in the image of God. Jesus meant that the Pharisees were followers of Satan, disciples of Satan, figuratively "children" of Satan.

This is not the case in man's relationship with God. We bear his unmistakable mark, and too much cannot be made of this. We are his creation, his possession. So God cannot help but desire our welfare and not our ill. It is tragic that so many people, even believers, are afraid of God. If they could only realize that God does not want to hurt them or destroy them, their response to him would be altogether different. Nobody but the worst and most blind cynics can reject love and goodness when they fully realize that it is being offered.

Son

In contrast to the austerity picture some people have about God, many seem to think of Jesus as a mild, effeminate, weak sort of person who said a lot of good and wise things.

It is long past due that men realized that Jesus of Nazareth was and is the most incredible happening that has occurred in the universe. He is the focal point of all of the Father's orientation. Jesus is God. He is one with the Father, he said. But this is the fantastic thing: Jesus was human—absolutely, completely, and finally human. He is the only God-Human who has ever lived!

It was only in him that the awful price for men's sins could be paid. Among other things, this settles forever the intrinsic worth of men in the sight of the Father. Sins were human. The penalty for them must be exacted from humans or a Representative Human. But the penalty was infinite. Humans are finite. A representative human who was also the infinite God was necessary. Only Jesus could meet this demand. He met it satisfactorily.

The Son of God is the Savior of men. God has ordained that the benefits of his saviorhood are made available to those who will simply receive them in faith. The simplicity of this fact has been the most insurmountable obstacle for the minds of men. Jesus died, and God forgave those who would recognize and receive him. Jesus was resurrected and those who trust in him for eternal life receive it. Simple.

Finally, Jesus is the image toward which sinful men and women strive (we are still sinful even after conversion). The objective of Christian living is to be like Jesus. The more the believer's life becomes like the life of Christ, both when he walked this earth and even now in the Father's presence, the more the believer becomes spiritually mature.

Spiritual maturity is a process of "becoming." The therapist's efforts are concentrated on the counselee's place in that process. If the counselee is a nonbeliever, then this defines the first goal of the Christian therapist. It becomes the therapist's task to help him accept the fact that the answer to his problem lies in the direction of God.

Holy Spirit

The Holy Spirit shares with the Son and the Father those attributes that make God, God. He is a person and as such is just as personable as the Father, Son, or even any of us. The work of the Holy Spirit and his personality are generally the most underrated element of our understanding of God. We have academicized him, boxed him up, doctrinalized him, examined him, analyzed him, objectified him, and in short done everything but know him. We know very much about him. The Scripture is prolific in describing his Person and work. But our knowledge of him as a personality, and as a friend, is often inadequate.

The Holy Spirit regenerates a nonbeliever into a new creature in Christ, baptizes him, indwells him, and on occasion controls him.

This latter aspect is dependent upon the believer himself. The Scripture teaches that a believer can "quench" the Spirit of God. A spiritual Christian is one who walks in (is controlled by) the Spirit. One may be controlled by the Spirit when he is a baby in

Christ or when he is mature in his faith. Generally speaking, the frequency of this control in anyone's life is measured by the level of maturity of his Christian experience.

But these are theoretical factors. The most important thing about the Holy Spirit is that he too is on our side. He is our spiritual energy. He is our Motivator, our special Friend who is always with us no matter how gross our aberration or how strong our intimacy with the Father and Son. He is the one who provides the power for Christian living.

A second matter is of definitive importance in our concept of God. It has to do not only with *who he is,* as previously discussed, but with *what he is.* I think most of the credit for the austere concept of God must be laid at the feet of those who are very taken with his holiness. God is holy. Many consider this to be his primary function and moral attribute. In view of the fact that we are aware of our acute condition of sin, God's holiness, either objectively or subjectively, threatens us. We are afraid of God because he is holy and we are sinful. We cannot conceive of the fact that his holiness, which is so demanding, will not condemn us who are so sinful.

Now I want to say something at the risk of being horribly misunderstood: *The demands of God's holiness are not so great that they cannot be met and fulfilled by his love.* The Scripture tells us flatly that God is love. It was God's holiness that demanded a penalty and payment for sin. It was God's love that paid. *God met his own demands.* God met his own demands in himself. Presumably this was because he knew that we could not (because of our sin nature) meet those demands in ourselves. Notice, second, that the demands of God's holiness have already been met. For the believer, there are no more demands by God to conform to his holiness. If we are righteous, based on the fact that we were given the righteousness of Christ (2 Corinthians 5:21), the matter of the demands of a holy God is satisfied forever. Someone will doubtless remind me of 1 Peter 1:16, where it is demanded, "Be ye holy, for I am holy."

I don't argue that this statement was made to cleansed believers, but I do contend most earnestly that it has reference to the fact that I must continue in the process of maturing spiritually. My objective is conformity to the image of Christ (Romans 8:29). It is my objective, but it is God's work and it is his power that will bring it about (Philippians 2:13).

The demands of holiness have been met in the demands placed upon Jesus—which he paid. They are no longer a concern of mine as a believer. My sins, all of them, past, present, and future, have been forgiven. Sin is not to be the believer's preoccupation.

I have known and counseled with many Christians who can think of little else except their sin. This is not a holy attitude. It's a sick attitude, which has no basis whatsoever in Scripture. There is no reason for a Christian to have guilt feelings when the cause for that guilt has been forgiven.

Some will argue that I am confusing judicial forgiveness and imputed righteousness with the so-called demands for holy living. I want to say that I am doing exactly that. Only my choice of words would not be *confusing,* but *clarifying.* The "clarity" of my friends who object to what I am saying has served to create the situation that drives people to the psychologist's office. He tells them that their religion is damaging them and that they should forget it. You know something? I fully agree. Nothing could be so damaging to people's emotions in this pressure-cooker society than the awful bewilderment that results when one is supposed to be forgiven by God and yet in this life, when it really counts, he is not. This is hideous theology and deserves equally stringent condemnation from thinking Christians.

An individual's concept of God is critical. If he views God as an indiscriminate tyrant, if he views God as something or someone other than One who is genuinely concerned about his everyday problems and experiences, he is not going to respond positively to him. He may respond, and because of the novelty or the change, he will experience a measure of relief. But it will be short-lived. His misery will return, because his God is a God who demands of him what he cannot perform. If he does perform, he will not perform adequately. No sinful creature can be one whit holier than God sees fit to declare him. If he does not perform, he will be degraded or demeaned and pronounced bad. He will need someone to love him. Certainly his God does not.

God is not like this at all. If we are to extend help that has substance to it, we must help people to realize how deeply God really does love them. We must help them to realize that their misery is not some form of punishment from an exacting, austere Father. We must help them to realize that *God is not mad at them.*

9

SELF-IMAGE

Connected with our concept of God and almost equal to it is our concept of ourself. Everyone has emotional ups and downs. At times we all feel a little like David who remarked, "I am a worm and no man. . . ." But for people to feel like this as a matter of preoccupation, or worse, to really believe it, presents a case for spiritual and mental therapy.

I am deeply concerned that Christians are propagating a philosophy that is horribly demeaning to man. Most may deny that this is being done. Academically, we often refer to it as "Christian suffering" or following the footsteps of a "suffering Savior." However, in our comments about "the flesh," and in our "not I, but Christ" theology, and our "he must increase and I must decrease" mentality, and in many other similar expressions, we demean ourselves. Within a certain context, these statements of course are true. But in our attempts to apply them to experience, we distort their precise meaning. This is a sort of self-negation that Jesus never meant when he said that those who would follow him must take their cross and deny themselves. This approach to the human dilemma has not been a healthy one. It has in fact contributed heavily to the dilemma. Christians who rightly desire to please God, wrongly think that condemning themselves is part of pleasing him. It is no wonder that psychologists have concluded that a religionist (their name for us) is a masochist. We simply don't like ourselves. It is wonderful that God doesn't share our view.

MAN IN CREATION

What is man that thou art mindful of him? and the son of man, that thou visitest him? For thou hast made him a little lower than the angels, and hast crowned him with glory and honor. Thou madest him to have dominion over all the works of thy hands; thou hast put all things under his feet: All sheep and oxen, yea, and the beasts of the field; The fowl of the air, and the fish of the sea, and whatsoever passeth through the paths of the seas (*Psalm 8:4–8*).

When David wrote this, he had just finished reviewing the cosmos. It must have greatly impressed him. On a clear night, one can see several thousand stellar bodies. In our modern understanding of astronomy, the size of the universe has increased far beyond David's ability to imagine. It appears, however, that David was a bit overwhelmed. The questions that came to him were, "How do I fit into all of this?" "With all of this, why is God interested in me?"

Like many of us, David caught himself attempting to demean himself with the query, "What is man that thou art mindful of him?" It's important to note that if this was David's thinking, it didn't last for long. He immediately answers his own question. Observe what he included in his answer: God created him a "little lower than the angels." We are not to conclude that man is a lower form of creation than the angels, because this same statement is made of Christ (Hebrews 2:6–11). Doubtless unknown to David, this psalm of his finds messianic fulfillment. David meant it for himself.

Men were made lower than the angels in power certainly; also in the fact that unfallen angelic beings apparently have immediate access to the physical presence of God. Further, as this lower position was temporary with reference to Christ, so it will be with man (1 Corinthians 6:3). "Thou hast crowned him with glory and honor," etc.: this enumeration brings into relief the inadequacy of David's own understanding and amazement. David's problem was a paradox: How could man, a sinful creature, be given the control of all the glory that his eyes could see? David knew, nonetheless, that this was fact.

This passage teaches that not only was the earth to be made subject to the control of man, but the entirety of creation! I don't normally like to resort to speculation, but imagine with me what would be the situation if Adam had not liked fruit. We are all cognizant of the improprieties that we have forced upon our planet. Pollution of air, water, and land have brought dire predictions: mathematical projections indicate possible dissolution of the human race if the present trend is not arrested. Overpopulation is another stinging problem, which has led to liberalization of abortion laws, wide use of contraceptives, and a program to make them available to any who are capable of producing children. Educational programs are trying to influence people not to have more than two children per married couple, and on and on it goes. Now think of where we would be if Adam were still alive and replenishing the earth! Wouldn't this be precisely the case had he not sinned and brought death into the world along with the curse? How fast would men have progressed without the curse of sin to retard the brain? When in the course of human history would man have reached the moon if we didn't have to contend with a blighted spirit? It makes you think, doesn't it?

When God formed Adam from the dust of the earth, he brought forth a being unlike any other in the universe. Of all the created beings this one was most like himself. This one had the power to choose good and evil. He had the prerogative to go his own way. God had not made anything or anyone like that. After it was all done, *he pronounced it good.*

The first man in his perfect condition could interact with God on a unique basis. It is implied that God enjoyed this kind of relationship. In Genesis 3 we are told that he was in the garden in "the cool of the day," presumably to interact with Adam on a casual basis. Adam was nowhere to be found. He had blown the whole thing, for all of us.

Today we humans still bear the mark of the image of God. God still desires the same kind of dignified relationship with us that he had with Adam before he sinned. God had intended great things for us: a whole universe to conquer and enjoy. But our sinful condition has blurred the perfect image of God which once we bore, though the basics are still there. There is enough worth to us to cause God still to care.

MAN ON EARTH IN TIME

For millennia now, man has existed by the sweat of his brow. He has been contending with a condition he brought upon himself. Through the years he has tried and tried to cleanse himself and in some way to reach God again. He has fabricated gods. He has penalized himself and in countless ways worked to appease what deep down in his heart he knows is awry. He has failed. All appears hopeless.

Why did God create man? If he is omniscient he must have known that this would take place. True, he must have known. God has not chosen to reveal to men what his basic motivations were in creation. I refuse to accept the dogma that God created man so he could have something to worship him. The Scripture nowhere teaches this. We aren't God's plaything, his pet poodle, his toy. I suppose it could be said that Sally, my golden retriever, worships me. But this isn't the kind of relationship that God desires with me. I believe that God wants of me today the kind of relationship he enjoyed with Adam before he sinned, only better and more intimate. This is seen in the influence that Christ has made upon my reconciliation with the Father. God, when he created the human race, must have had in his infinite and magnificent mind the establishment of a Divine Family, where each loved and respected each other out of the sheer willful desire to do so.

When man ruined this, God set about cleaning up the mess by reestablishing the relationship and making it better. This is what he is doing now. God is operating in and through men today. He is concerned for them and is reaching out to them in a way compatible with his nature and attributes. This is, of course, the purpose of the God-Man. In Jesus Christ, the Father penetrated the problem of human sin in the only effective way. In Jesus Christ we see God, his holiness and his love and compassion for those whom he made and set in motion. God still wants his family. He is determined to get it.

10

THE BELIEVER'S POSITION IN CHRIST

The Christian's "position in Christ" is perhaps the most important concept that can be communicated in therapy. It is extremely important that the therapist understands it well.

When a human responds affirmatively to God, something occurs that can be understood only as a supernatural intervention by God into the affairs and course of that individual's living experience. God loves. Men, women, teenagers, and children respond to that love by returning it through faith in the object provided for our love: the Son of God.

Not only is Jesus the object of our love, it is through him and in him that we are accepted by God. When the right response to God's love is made, the believer involuntarily assumes a mystical but real posture that identifies him with the second person of the Godhead. This posture is described in Scripture as being "in Christ." Ephesians 1 mentions this position no less than nine times. This particular chapter is one of the most significant in all of the

Word of God, especially to the believer. It warrants our consideration of certain key ideas:

> Blessed be the God and Father of our Lord Jesus Christ,
> who has blessed us with all spiritual blessings in heavenly
> places in Christ *(Ephesians 1:3).*

One of the most exciting things about being "in Christ" is that it brings with it all spiritual blessings that are "in the heavenly places." The word used for "blessing" in this case is *eulogia,* which means essentially to "speak well of." In other words, God has blessed us with all "good speaking" in the heavenly places. The location "in heavenly places" may mean that when we get to heaven he will speak well of us, or he is now in heaven speaking well of us. Because we are in Christ, *there is nothing that God finds which he can condemn.* The only thing he can see or say is "good." This should help us in our understanding of how God views us in the course of our present experiences. He does not depreciate us. Why should we depreciate ourselves? We are "in Christ"!

Don't make the mistake of thinking that this applies only to the glorified state of the believer and not to his present life now. Many theologians have a tendency so to compartmentalize God's dealings with men that they fail to see that, whatever God is going to give us in the way of qualitative blessings, we now possess. I'm not suggesting perfectionism of human conduct and behavior in this life, but I am suggesting that God does not punitively view the sin in the believer's life.

> . . . he hath chosen us in him before the foundation of the
> world, that we should be holy and without blame before
> him . . . (*Ephesians 1:4*).

This verse stresses that each believer was chosen by God before the establishment of the cosmos. There was a time when time began. At some point time will end. Chronology will become obsolete and finally extinct. It is impossible for us to divorce our minds from time orientation, but we are told that at some point in eternity, whether seconds or eternities before time began, God thought of us.

He knew in advance who our parents would be. He knew our ancestors as well as he knew us. He *knew* each moment, each second, each millisecond of our lives. He knew the day, the hour, the moment of our conversion. And because God knows that something will take place at a given moment in time, it is *absolutely* certain that it will come to pass at that moment, not a second before or after. This is an *unalterable* law. God knows when things will take place, and because of this knowledge, they *must of necessity* take place at that time.

This does not abrogate human responsibility. It merely says that God knows beforehand the choices we will make as a result of our own exercise of will. Therefore from his point of view the choices are inevitable and as unchangeable as his knowledge.

While this does not relieve us of responsibility, it does give the confidence that he is in control of our lives. No decision will be made without his knowledge and understanding. This is certainly one of the reasons why Paul remarked, ". . . I know whom I have believed, and am persuaded that he is able to keep that which I have committed unto him against that day" (2 Timothy 1:12).

"Having predestinated us unto the adoption of children . . ." (Ephesians 1:5).

This is incredible. This is what we were speaking of earlier when we discussed that fact about God desiring a family for himself. The concept of adoption here does not follow the modern concept, but the one in use among Hebrew peoples in Paul's day and before. There was a time when a Hebrew child would come of age. At that time he was "placed as a son." We are not to understand here that we are orphans and that we are to be adopted who were the children of other parents. We are born of God, but at the same time, upon glorification we will be placed as "sons." In connection with this idea is Ephesians 1:22, 23,

> . . . and gave him to be the head over all things to the church, which is his body, the fullness of him that filleth all in all.

This passage tells us that the Church is the *fullness* of Christ. Think of the enormous implications of that. Jesus fills all in all—

and *we fill him!* The language of Scripture indicates that we are part of the Son. We shall one day enjoy a sonship identified with him. One cannot help but think of the old geometric syllogism: Things equal to the same thing are equal to each other.

Now note another passage in this connection:

> For now we see in a mirror dimly, but then face to face; now I know in part, but then I shall know fully just as I also have been fully known (1 Corinthians 13:12).

The pieces of the puzzle are beginning to become more clear. Paul is saying that in this life he is essentially inadequate, but in the next life he will know—note carefully—he will know as fully as he is now known by God. Does this suggest that upon glorification Paul's knowledge will be infinite? How well does God know Paul? Paul is saying that his future knowledge will be measured by that.

One final passage is the capstone to what we are trying to express here:

> Beloved, now we are the sons of God, and it doth not appear what we shall be: but we know that, when he shall appear, we shall be like him; for we shall see him as he is (1 John 3:2).

No man has ever seen with physical eyes the unrestrained glory of God and lived. But one day we shall. And the statement that arrests my attention here is, "We shall be like him . . ."

We shall be identified with him and be like him, yet the individuality of each one of us will be maintained. Our freedom of choice will still be our own, even with the incredible knowledge that Paul spoke of possessing. God's family will be complete and finalized.

This ought to do something for our self-image.

We believers are prone to be critical of each other and of ourselves. We must remember that we are on an assembly line. If we could view each other as God views us, we would never criticize each other. We would view each other as perfect. But for the moment, I would like to suggest that we follow the advice of Bill Gothard: "Please be patient; God is not finished with me yet!"

The Christian counselee will be greatly helped if he comes into the emotional realization of how much God really thinks of him.

He must realize that his problems are temporary, that God has specifically and meaningfully allowed them or directed them for a constructive purpose.

> And we know that God causes all things to work together for good to those who love God, to those who are called according to His purpose (*Romans 8:28, NASB*).

This doesn't say that all things are good or right or pleasant or unpleasant, but it does assure us that no experience of life must inevitably work to our detriment as believers.

I know very few ministers who preach this. Most want to modify Romans 8:28 in some way. This is because most are sin-oriented. We must account for sin!

I say we must *not* account for sin! God accounted for it, past tense, with present and future effect. Romans 8:28 flatly indicates that no matter what we do, no matter how great our sin, the ultimate result of it for the believer is good. It is an integral process of attaining the image of Christ.

Now before my reader discards this work as bordering on heresy, let me say that I am in full accord with Paul who said, "Shall we sin . . . that grace may abound? God forbid." God does not want the believer to sin, and he must make every effort not to. But if he does, "Grace much more abounds." This is another way of saying that God's grace is greater than our sin: he has taken into account that we are sinners. Exactly how God's grace affects the fact of our sinful behavior will be discussed later with respect to forgiveness. But for now let us state that there is no sin which a believer has committed that God's grace has not already covered.

11

FORGIVENESS

What we are doing in Part III is making an effort to rid ourselves of long-held attitudes about God and our relationship to him. The reason for this is that what most Christians believe about these matters has worked more toward mental slavery and bondage than it has provided what Jesus promised: freedom. He said, "Ye shall know the truth and the truth shall make you free." But for many Christians today, freedom means adhering to "God's standard of conduct." In fact, it is more often the standard of conduct imposed upon them by those who hold medieval concepts of theology. I am not using *medieval* by way of insult, but I am simply saying that Christianity today is sometimes characterized by sub-biblical views that arose during the Dark Ages.

The Christian's concept of forgiveness is a classic example of this. The popular view is that while the believer has been forgiven of his sin because of what Christ did at Calvary, he nonetheless must *yet* be forgiven for the sins he commits daily. The idea is that when we sin, we lose our fellowship with God and must be reinstated by a process of "confession" which prompts God to forgive us. Some have attached a label to this process and it has been widely accepted by lay people and clergy alike.

This position seems to me the result of misunderstanding. Its illogical aspects have never, to my satisfaction at least, been explained. If God has forgiven *all* my sins, why does he have to forgive them again? To put it another way, if all my sins have been forgiven, and if by *all* is meant every sin I have ever committed, i.e., current sins, and all the sins I have yet to commit in this life: if all of these have been forgiven based upon the atonement (Ephesians 1:7), why is it necessary for God to engage himself in further acts of forgiveness? Nothing is left to forgive! The answer to this question is, of course, it *isn't* necessary. This one logical objection alone fatally wounds the aforementioned position.

The misunderstanding of which I spoke is to a large extent a misunderstanding of 1 John 1:9:

> If we confess our sins, He is faithful and righteous to forgive us our sins and to cleanse us from all unrighteousness *(NASB)*.

A superficial interpretation of this verse concludes that the forgiveness is based upon the individual's confessing. A very serious problem with this conclusion is: Suppose we don't confess; do we enter heaven unforgiven? Or worse, do we enter heaven at all? Most interpreters try to skirt this objection by saying that the forgiveness has reference to fellowship, not to salvation. Two important considerations render this evasion untenable: (1) The word *fellowship* does not appear in the statement. (2) The verse is plainly talking about forgiveness of sin. The consequences of unforgiven sin must not be watered down to mean something less than spiritual death.

Another common evasion of the problems this interpretation presents is that it has reference only to known sin. This seems to me to be the most absurd thinking of all. If this were true, what about the unknown sin? Is lack of cognizance with respect to sinful acts a valid excuse to allow them exemption from penalty? Also, how much time is permitted to elapse between the act of sin and its confession? Suppose the believer dies before the act is confessed? Is some kind of theological "statute of limitations" suggested by this verse? (I remember that in college this question formed the basis of serious debate in our theological "bull sessions" among ministerial students. It's ridiculous. Such an interpretation presents logical absurdities and unanswerable questions which make the discussion almost laughable.)

What follows is what I believe to be a more realistic understanding of 1 John 1:9.

First, the word *confess* is not to be understood to mean that the believer is revealing anything to God. God is well aware of the sins we commit, even before we commit them. The idea behind this word is not *to reveal,* but *to agree.* The implication is that when we sin, we should agree with God that what we have done was indeed wrong or sinful.

Second, the Scripture nowhere teaches that a believer can be "out of fellowship." None of the writers of the Bible speaks of being "in fellowship" or "out of fellowship" with God in the widely accepted sense of that term. John has a number of comments to make about fellowship (1 John 1:3–7). He declares that "truly our fellowship *is* with the Father, and with his Son Jesus Christ." This is simply a statement of positional relationship which existed between John and his associates and God. Query: If John meant "on speaking terms," which is the implication of the common idea of fellowship, how could he have been so emphatic about the fellowship of those brethren captured in that little word "our"? Then must we conclude that John was writing only to believers and to no one else? Couldn't he have been writing to a church, or to a visible group of believers, or to the church in general, which doubtless included some who weren't genuinely regenerated? It seems to me that John was expressing his desire that all who were to come under the influence of his letter would join him and his friends in fellowship with God. He intended "fellowship" to mean the relationship that only a believer enjoys, synonymous with his position of being "in Christ."

If this is true, then a truly regenerated believer can no more be "out of fellowship" than he can be "out of Christ." After all, if our understanding of being in Christ is correct and if this position is static, how could one be more "in fellowship"? Jesus himself promised, "I am with you always, even to the end of the age."

Well then, what about the implied condition in 1 John 1:9? "If we confess . . . he is faithful . . ." If we do not confess, is God not faithful? We know that he is. May I suggest that the word *if* does not always imply condition in its strictest sense. In James 5:15, we observe that

> . . . if [a man] have committed sins, they shall be forgiven him . . .

The *if* here does not raise the question as to whether or not the man has committed sins. All men have committed sins. The *if* is to imply a state of existing condition. I believe the same can be said for 1 John 1:9. John uses the word *if* five times in this passage to indicate various nuances of status. No verse of Scripture stands alone. It must be understood in the light of other passages bearing upon the same subject. With this in mind, let us translate verses 6–10 as follows:

> If we are saying that we have communion with him and are walking in darkness, we lie, and are not doing the truth. But since we are walking in the light, as he is in the light, we have communion with each other, and the blood of Jesus Christ his Son is continuing to cleanse us from all sin. If we are saying that we have no sin, we deceive ourselves and the truth is not in us. Since we agree to our sins, he is faithful and just in order to forgive us our sins and cleanse us from all unrighteousness. If we say that we have not sinned, we make him a liar, and his word is not in us.

The fact that a believer has been already forgiven prohibits us from concluding that he would not be forgiven if he did not confess. Paul's first letter to the Corinthians (11:31, 32) provides further help:

> For if we would judge ourselves, we should not be judged. But when we are judged, we are chastened of the Lord, that we should not be condemned with the world.

When a believer agrees that he has sinned, he has formed a correct judgment about himself and has forestalled any corrective measures by God. If he does not confess, i.e., agree that he has sinned, when he most certainly has sinned, God brings into play the correction process spoken of in Hebrews 12:3–13. The correction therefore will always be in direct relation to the sin in question. The believer will not be in the dark about the reason he is being corrected, nor will he be in any doubt about the fact that he is indeed being corrected. If this is what is meant by "known sin," then we concur.

The forgiveness spoken of in 1 John 1:9 means that God "forgives" the person who confesses to the extent that he withholds correction. It probably should be said as well that any believer who confesses is sincere only to the degree that he does not wish to sin again and makes positive effort not to do so. It must be remembered too that when God corrects a believer, he never does it in anger or wrath, but is motivated by love and concern for the welfare of his child.

Unconfessed sin is a deliberate and premeditated act. One cannot unwittingly avoid agreeing with God that he has sinned. Unconfessed sin is not an indication that a person is out of fellowship. But it does indicate that he is harboring evil, thus grieving the Holy Spirit and forfeiting his control. However, as an act of love, God will bring him through correction to the point where he surrenders his own will to that of the Holy Spirit. Once again it will be God who works in him both to will and to do of his good pleasure (Philippians 2:13).

12

THE MINISTRY OF
THE HOLY SPIRIT

We have already said some things about the Holy Spirit as a personality who resides within each believer, wholly distinct from the personality either of the Father or of the believer himself.

HOLY SPIRIT BAPTISM

Much has been written about this subject and I don't intend to labor it further here. But I do want to clarify what is meant by it. The controlling passage with respect to Spirit baptism must of necessity be 1 Corinthians 12:13. There we are told exactly who is baptized by him:

> For by one Spirit *we are all baptized into one body* . . . and have been all made to drink into one Spirit.

This passage clearly states that all believers have been baptized with the Holy Spirit.

The first Spirit baptism occurred on the Day of Pentecost, recorded for us in Acts 2. This was when the "Church Age" began. This was when the Body of Christ was first formed. From that point to this day, when a person becomes a believer in Christ by faith, he is baptized by the Spirit of God and is regenerated. The tense of the verb in the passage above indicates that there is only one Spirit baptism in the life of a believer.

INDWELLING OF THE SPIRIT

> . . . your body is a temple of the Holy Ghost which is in you, which ye have of God (*1 Corinthians 6:19*).

Believers are regenerated and baptized by the Spirit of God. He never leaves them. In fact, he takes up his residence within the life and experience and "body" of the believer. He is that divine nature which leads the child of God into the paths of righteousness and produces the "fruit of the Spirit." What a magnificent thing to know that God is in us! The God who commanded light to shine out of darkness, who spoke the planets into existence, and who directs the course of human events is in us. He has promised to remain there for eternity. This makes the believer in Jesus Christ as indestructible as God himself.

When I was a very young Christian, I asked a minister whom I respected and followed, how one is *filled* with the Spirit. He told me that to be filled with the Word of God was to be filled with the Spirit of God. Frankly, I think that this was very good advice to a young believer not very well grounded in the Scripture. He knew that if this requirement was met, the other would follow. He was a very wise pastor indeed.

THE FILLING OF THE SPIRIT

Basically, to be *filled with the Spirit means to be controlled by him.* We therefore function in response to his direction. It is not a crisis experience. It is a way of living, a process by which we are to one degree or another positively influenced by him. Of course, his direction cannot be objectively known without the Divine

Record. The filling of the Spirit has a subjective or mystical aspect to it as well. Under the control of the Spirit, the believer will make decisions affecting the everyday experiences of his life, about which the Bible has no direct word.

I think it unfortunate that many teach that the Bible has an answer for every circumstance in life—meaning that it can give guidance and direction about all the decisions one must make, no matter how trivial or innocuous. It does not tell me whether I should buy a blue suit or brown. It does not tell me what brand of coffee to like. The point is, countless decisions in life God expects us to make on our own, relying upon the mystical, subjective guidance from the Holy Spirit and upon our human intelligence to keep us from error.

The Spirit directly influences at least three basic areas of experience:

(1) *The fruit of the Spirit:* The "fruits" of the Spirit are listed for us in Galatians 5:22, 23. They are very important and should be individually studied and meditated upon. Note that the very first mentioned is *love.* I am going to talk about love in detail in the next chapter, but I wish to stress its importance here as well.

One of the greatest problems of church people is their inability to relate to each other on a one-to-one basis. The reason for this is that we do not know how to love. Many pastors say that they love their people, but ask the person in the pew if he feels that the pastor loves him. No? (I can hear the pastor respond gruffly, mumbling remarks about "dissidents," or "he just doesn't appreciate me," or "he has sin in his life.") The oceans of criticism that church members receive from one another is an infallible barometer of the nature of the "love" being expressed. Lack of this fruit of the Spirit is one of the saddest blights upon the church of Jesus Christ today.

Building in a counselee or patient the ability to love is probably the most important contribution a therapist can make to his life. Closely related to it is the fruit of the Spirit, listed next, *joy.* Joy does not mean a constant state of elation. But it does mean that fundamental strata of happiness and contentment can underlie one's unalterable lot in life. Things that can be altered can be viewed as a happy challenge, not as dismal drudgery.

In short, the fruits of the Spirit provide those qualities of life that make for a well-adjusted, non-problem-oriented individual. One can readily see their value.

(2) The second area of experience influenced by the control of the Spirit is *our internal motivation and power.* Three passages in Ephesians describe the phenomena produced in the life of the believer who is governed by the Spirit:

> . . . that ye may know . . . what is the exceeding greatness of his power to us-ward who believe, according to the working of his mighty power, which he wrought in Christ when he raised him from the dead . . . (*1:18–20*). . . . whereof I was made a minister, according to the gift of the grace of God given unto me by the effectual working of his power . . . (*3:7*). That he would grant you, according to the riches of his glory, to be strengthened with might by his Spirit in the inner man [*the Unconscious*], that Christ may dwell in your hearts by faith; that ye, being rooted and grounded in love, may be able to comprehend with all saints what is the breadth, and length, and depth, and height; and to know the love of Christ, which passeth knowledge, that ye might be filled with all the fulness of God. Now unto him that is able to do exceeding abundantly above all that we ask or think, according to the power that worketh in us . . . (*3:16–20*).

One thing the secular academic community cannot explain is the phenomenological occurrences that take place in human affairs contrary to normal established sequences of events. For example, medicine's cure for drug addiction is at best an involved process; and if withdrawal symptoms are precipitated, it is extremely painful. But the power of God working in the life of the one who has been regenerated releases the individual completely, in some cases, from any symptoms of withdrawal. One moment his addiction is positive. The next moment it is negative. In other cases, a man comes under the power and control of the Spirit of God and his perennial problem of alcoholism is gone. Terminal and lesser cases of cancer mysteriously disappear. The patient claims to have an intimate relationship with God, and that God healed him. Can anyone step forward and contradict him? Can a better explanation be suggested? A timid, introverted, weak-willed individual discovers the power of God within him and it's as if he were given a totally new personality. He becomes strong, aggressive, and confident. His influence with others seems almost irresistible.

These testimonies and the Scripture cited tell us that when a human being comes under the control of the Holy Spirit, he becomes motivated and powerful in his pursuits. Obstacles seem to fall away with seemingly little effort on his part. Or the "power" may not be anywhere near so spectacular. It may evidence itself in a quiet spirit of resilience and strength. But it's there, surging through the heart and mind and being of the child of God.

(3) The third area of a believer's experience that results from the control of the Spirit is the phenomenon of *spiritual or charismatic gifts.* These gifts are listed in Ephesians 4:11, 12; 1 Peter 4:9–11; Romans 12:3–8; and 1 Corinthians 12–14. It is not my purpose to enumerate them here, but I wish to emphasize their importance and the necessity of their discovery and use in relation to the spiritual and mental health of the counselee.

The Scripture teaches that each believer has one or more "gifts," which are to be used for self and church edification. They are to be distinguished from talents, in the sense that both believers and nonbelievers possess certain talents. Spiritual gifts are used to communicate God's blessings and benefits to one another. Between seventeen and twenty-two of these gifts are mentioned in the passages just cited. It's possible that there may be more, not mentioned *per se* in Scripture. Any activity that (a) serves the purpose of edification and (b) requires a certain capacity or ability to perform is correctly identified as a "charismatic gift."

Because charismatic gifts have not received much attention from the church at large, the church has suffered. Before I began to teach this doctrine to my own congregation, if I were to ask someone what they thought their spiritual gift might be, their reaction would probably be puzzled. This is not a widely discussed subject and, as a result, believers in general are not well taught in these matters.

It must be remembered that the fullness of the Spirit can operate only within the believer's knowledge of the Word. This is not to say that many believers are not unwittingly exercising their "gifts," but they seem limited in doing so. Therapists, therefore, must help their counselee to discover his gift or gifts. This in and of itself provides constructive and corrective therapy.

We have yet to answer the question, "How can one be filled with the Spirit?" I'm aware that others have answered this question adequately, but permit me to offer a contribution that may help some people.

In Colossians 2:6 we note,

As ye have therefore received Christ Jesus the Lord, so walk ye in him.

We are told as well to "walk in the Spirit . . ." "Walk," of course, means the deportment of life. We know that the filling of the Spirit of God is an intermittent thing, but it should not be. Our "walk" should be characterized by it. Now note the words, "As ye have received Christ . . . so walk . . ." If we were to ask the question "How do I receive Christ?" we would answer "By faith." Is it too difficult to understand, then, that we are to be controlled by the Spirit of God in the same way? It is simple to believe in Christ. It is likewise simple to be controlled by the Spirit.

People in general make too much out of the concept of being filled with the Spirit. They often feel that they must "do something"—preferably something spectacular. All one has to do to receive the filling of the Spirit is the same thing he had to do to receive Christ: *believe!* What an incredible word. What an impossible word. Believe. Why is it so hard to say yes to the Spirit, and then to believe that he responded to the yes in the same way that Christ responds to it? Our lack of belief defeats us, the same as it does when we don't believe in Christ. If we invite the Spirit to control us and refuse to believe that he does it, then we have sinned, and he indeed has not functioned. The Holy Spirit responds to belief—not works—just as Jesus did when we believed that he saved us.

This brings us to the final consideration. Here I want to discuss those areas of life's experiences when we are not controlled. The Spirit of God can be "grieved" and he can be "quenched" (Ephesians 4:30; 1 Thessalonians 5:19). This occurs when we sin. Remember, "whatsoever is not of faith is sin . . ." When we fail to believe, we sin, and the Spirit is grieved/quenched. We are not under his control. How do we un-grieve and un-quench him again?

We must agree with God that what we have done is wrong (1 John 1:9).

As a matter of fact, for the most part, Christians need not even give the filling of the Spirit much thought at all. The Spirit of God will give us assurance that he is controlling our life through his mystical witness and through the fruits spoken of in Galatians. Confidence and belief are the key.

13

HOW TO LOVE

One of the most meaningful experiences of my life as a Christian and as a child of God is the joy of loving and of being loved. When I was first introduced to the Lord in the living room of my employer, I felt real genuine love for the first time in my life that I could remember. I realized that these dear people who were telling me about Christ really loved me. When I was first brought to church as a brand new Christian, age twenty, I discovered that there were other people too who really loved and cared for me.

It wasn't long, however, before I discovered that these people were not perfect, and that their love was equally imperfect. I have stated that probably the biggest problem facing members of the church today is their inability to relate in love to each other. Believers come to church, sit in the pew, hear the sermon, and relate individually to God—but not to the ones who are worshiping with them. Preachers of the gospel, usually suffering from a Moses or Elijah complex, thunder rebuke and threatenings from the pulpit. The hearers either identify with him and share in his enthusiasm, become frightened of him and his fire-eating god, or turn him off altogether. My first pastorate taught me more about my relationships with God's people than eight years of higher education. I was one who thundered, pounded, shouted, and flayed. I was very pious in my assertion that I loved my people—but somehow, among all the messages they were receiving from me, they weren't getting that one. A guest speaker came one Sunday in my absence, and later, when I asked one of my members how the people received him, I was informed quite candidly that one parishioner had remarked that this was the first time since I'd come there that he didn't leave church feeling he'd just been chewed out. The parishioner in question was a man whom I thought was one of my most faithful supporters. Indeed he was! That remark was one of the biggest favors he could have done for me.

I didn't last much longer with that congregation. I left under a cloud. I was just finishing my final semester in seminary, so for the remainder of the semester I worked as an assistant to another pastor nearby. It was here that the next step in my education in love came about. The pastor here had long experience and his influence among his people was obvious. They all loved him, as far as I could tell, and yet he wielded a profound effect upon the church as a whole. Somehow, in a way that I couldn't explain or analyze at the time, his people knew and felt that he loved them.

This was my problem in my previous pastorate. The people felt that I didn't love them. Some, of course, didn't feel this way, but apparently most did. Now those who did were wrong. I did love them. But I had failed to communicate it. I don't mean by this that I failed to express it, but I failed to *communicate* it. Communication involves one who is sending and one who is receiving. I was sending, but on the wrong frequency for most people.

Love hasn't been communicated if it hasn't been felt in the life and heart of the object loved. This is what I had to learn. Virtually all people respond to love. It is one of the basic needs of man. The lover must keep on loving, and trying different ways of loving, until he strikes a responsive chord. Then he has communicated. I don't know that I have communicated love until Algernon Anthrax says, "I know the pastor loves me because I feel it." Love, along with everything else that it is, is most certainly emotional.

I had studied "love" in the Bible in school, and I felt I knew what it was all about. But here again, I found out something about academics and the Scripture. *One of the fundamental precepts of interpretive principles is that the Bible is pragmatic.* That is, it is workable in experience. If we come to some academic conclusion about biblical truth, which we then find difficult or impossible to put into practice, the odds are in favor of reevaluating our academics. We need to study that conclusion again and again, until we see how it works in life. I feel strongly about this. I believe that if our formulated doctrine having to do with life experience is not workable in that experience, then the doctrine is false and therefore dangerous. *This is the problem with most aberrant behavior among believers. They don't understand God or the Bible within the framework of life experience.*

My study of love in the Scripture has dramatically affected my life and the complexion of my ministry. Both are indescribably more satisfying and rewarding. I now feel as if I can love without inhibition, rigidity, or restraint. As a matter of fact, love has become so real to me that social propriety has become frustrating.

An analytical, academic approach to Scripture is essential if one is to arrive at the scientific truth of the Word. But all too often scholars approach the Book scientifically only to arrive at conclusions untenable in the crucible of life. Such efforts haven't been wasted, to the extent that one need not feel that he should expend the same effort again. In the case of the study of love, such an approach is immensely fruitful to life.

The word *love,* in the English language at least, is abused. People love people, sweethearts, dogs, cats, and candy. Someone may "just love" to do something he has never done. The Greeks did not express love in this fashion. They used an assortment of words to identify concepts, attitudes, and emotions which we identify with just one word. (Sometimes one Greek word will express what it takes many English words to say, and vice versa.) The various nuances of *love* are expressed in numerous ways in Greek.

The New Testament was written in the language that was on the lips of everyone in that day. They were speaking it long before the New Testament was written and continued to do so long after. However, it's worthwhile to note that the common (*koine*) Greek merely provided a vocabulary that the Holy Spirit would use while employing the personality and mentality of the various writers. That this "employment" borders on the spectacular is witnessed by the change in the personality of the Apostle Peter after he was baptized and controlled by the Spirit. Prior to Pentecost, Peter was an "ignorant and unlearned man." But afterward he held his own with the best of them. This is mentioned to suggest that the Holy Spirit certainly was not rigidly bound by the use, syntax, and definitions prevalent in the common language. Grammar, except to purist grammarians, is far from an exacting science anyway. Definitions of words were then just as fluid and fleeting as they are today. But once recorded in Scripture, a defined word becomes crystallized and identified by the way in which it is used and in the context in which it is found, and by other texts bearing upon the same subjects.

The Greeks apparently popularized at least four words that we today designate as *love*. The first we shall consider here is the word *eros*. This is the word from which we get our word *erotic*. The Greeks understood *eros* to mean "romantic love." One of its features was that it was intrinsically temporal in nature. Without nourishment, *eros* would die in time. It needed a deeper commitment to survive for very long. *Eros* is nowhere to be found in Scripture. This is not to suggest that romantic love is ignored in the Bible; it simply isn't expressed by that word.

The second word is *storge*. This word is found twice in the New Testament. Paul used it in his letter to the Romans (1:31; 12:10). In both cases it is used with a prefix. Its basic meaning is not clear, but apparently it has to do with "natural affection." Perhaps it could be equated with a sense of mutual respect among fellow men. In 1:31 it is translated "without natural affection," and in 12:10 it is translated "kindly affectioned."

The third word that the Greek people commonly used for love was *phileo*. This word was used to express friendship, brotherly love, or emotional affection, and in this latter sense was kin to *eros*. The word is used in the New Testament to express "kiss" three times.

By far the most widely used word for love in the New Testament is *agape*. This word represented the relationship between a mother and her child, or a similar relationship. *Agape* involves more than any other kind of love. It involves capitulation and commitment to the one loved. It is used in the New Testament no less than 256 times (including its noun and verb forms).

Thus the Greeks thought of love in at least four different ways; there were four different "kinds" of love. The husband-wife relationship may be seen to run in progression: from *storge* (mutual respect), to *eros* (romantic love), to *phileo* (deeper emotional affection), and finally, *agape* (genuine concern for the welfare of the loved one to the point of complete personal sacrifice).

How does this affect our understanding of what the New Testament teaches about love? So far as I am able to understand, Jesus left us only two commands, which in turn summarized all of the imperatives of the Bible. Those commands are (1) to believe, and (2) love (1 John 3:23). Some have concluded that a command to love cannot be obeyed, since love is an emotion and cannot be turned on and off at will. Some answer this objection, or shall I say frustration, by suggesting that Jesus commanded us to have *agape*, not *phileo*, which can be obeyed because *agape* is produced by the will. This suggestion would be in line with the King James use of the word *charity* for love in 1 Corinthians 13 and elsewhere, since *agape* is genuine concern for the beneficial welfare of others to the point of self-sacrifice. Others support this concept by saying, "How can you love someone you don't even like?" The answer to their problem is found in this rather comfortable interpretation of *agape*.

I am forced to reject these problems and their respective solutions because I find them either academically irresponsible or experientially untenable. Further, I contend that the Greek use of the words *agape* and *phileo* has little influence upon how they are used in the Scripture and their subsequent interpretations. The solutions above really solve no problems. They attempt to skirt them and as a result actually cause more difficulty than they solve.

I want to concentrate now upon just how the Scripture uses these two words for love.

PHILEO

Certain passages in which this word is used indicate that its basic intent is emotional affection. It was used to describe our Lord's love for Lazarus, which moved him to tears (John 11:3, 36). Also it is

used in connection with the special affection which Jesus held for
John the "beloved" apostle (John 20:2). It was the word Peter used
to express his affection to Christ (John 21:15–17). Other passages
indicate that *phileo* was used to express what we refer to as Christian love (Titus 3:15). This word, however, is also used in connection with love of family in contrast with love for God (Matthew
10:37); inanimate things (Matthew 6:5; 23:6; Luke 20:46); and it
is used for man's love for God (1 Corinthians 16:22).[1]

AGAPE

Since *agape* occurs many times in Scripture, I shall not follow
a similar process with it as for *phileo.* Let me only say that *agape*
is used to express the love of the Father for the Son, the Son for
the Father, God for man, man for God, man for man, Christian
for Christian, man for woman, and finally, love for inanimate
things.

The relation that *phileo* has with *agape* deserves some attention,
since in every way that *phileo* is used, *agape* is also used. I would
like to suggest, therefore, that the biblical use of these words does
not make the distinction between them that the Greeks did. In
Scripture, it can readily be seen that *agape* and *phileo* don't represent two kinds of love. It would be more accurate to say that the
two words represented two facets of the same thing, though even
this distinction isn't always clear. It would appear from its broad
use in Scripture that *agape* is the larger of the two forms. It seems
to me that *agape* is so broad that it absorbs the respective meanings
of *phileo, storge,* and *eros. Phileo,* on the other hand, is more
specific. It seems to carry with it more of the aspect of "affection,"
viz., the case of Jesus weeping for Lazarus. But it is important to
note that *agape* is likewise used to denote affection. We are told
that Jesus loved (*agape*) Martha and her sister and Lazarus (John
11:5).

The most classic passage where these two words interact is the
time after the Resurrection when Jesus was dining with the disci-

1. In this last connection W. L. Walker, author of the article on this subject in the
International Standard Bible Encyclopedia, disagrees. He states: "*Phileo* ... is
never used in Scripture language to designate man's love for God." It might surprise
Mr. Walker that *phileo* is also used to describe God's love for man (John 16:27).

ples on the shores of Galilee. Jesus turned to Peter and said, "Simon, son of Jonas, lovest thou me?" (*agape*) Peter responded with the assertion, "Lord, thou knowest I love thee!" (*phileo*) Jesus repeated the question again, using *agape*. Peter responded with *phileo*. Then Jesus put the same question to Peter again, this time using Peter's expression, *phileo*.

Almost all expositors when analyzing this passage point out that Peter was using an "inferior" word for love, simply indicating his "fondness" for the Lord. Such a conclusion is not fair to Peter, nor does it reveal a perceptive understanding of the man. Far more than all the other disciples, Peter was a passionate man. I don't need to prove this. Even a casual acquaintance with Peter's life makes this clear. Far from using an inferior word for love, Peter was expressing the fervency of his love for Christ. As far as Peter was concerned, he was using the more specific, the more passionate, the more meaningful word. That this is true is witnessed by the fact that our Lord never rebuked Peter for his use of the "inferior" word; indeed, on the third occasion, he used it himself.

Now we note something about this scene that I have never encountered in any class I've taken, in any sermon I've heard on this passage, or in any book or commentary with which I've had experience. When our Lord concedes to Peter's wish to use *phileo*, John, who is recording the scene, interjects a comment about Peter's emotional response to the third question. He informs us that Peter was grieved because Jesus said to him the *third* time, "Lovest thou me?" (*phileo*) There is one obvious problem with this statement: it isn't true! Jesus used *phileo* only once, not three times. And yet John says that he used it three times. This can only mean that John recognized little if any difference between the two words. It may be said that he considered them synonymous.

All of these considerations of the use of *phileo* and *agape* in the Scripture have led me to believe that *agape* is *love inclusive*. One cannot have *agape* without *phileo*. One cannot love in the way that Jesus loved without involving the emotions. Possibly, one may have affection for someone without *agape*, but it's certain that one cannot have *agape* without *phileo*.

One cannot truly love without affection. I think that this is what I was trying to do in my first pastorate. I think this is what most Christians are doing when they come to church each Sunday. It may be what believers are doing within the confines of their own homes. It may be why kids are leaving "Christian homes" by the droves.

In answer to the question "How can I love someone I don't even like?" we must reply "You can't." Or perhaps it's better to say that we must learn to distinguish between the person and his behavior, which may or may not be acceptable. This is crucial, if Christians are ever to be genuine, heartfelt lovers. We must learn to accept each other. We don't have to like the way a person acts, but we must love him with affection, and he must know it—or we're just faking the whole thing. We're as phony and as hypocritical as we can be. It's not enough to support worthy causes. It's not enough to give our money and our time to the church. We must give ourselves to each other. This is what Jesus meant when he said, "As I have loved you, so ye also love one another." It was his "new" commandment. It is a unique reality, possible only to those who are "in him."

We rigid, command-oriented, line-for-line and precept-upon-precept fundamentalists ought to learn what it is really to love with our hearts—unrestrained, unashamed, uninhibited love. Where did the holy kiss go? That wasn't a ritualistic thing. It wasn't the precursor of the "handshake." It wasn't a casual greeting. It was a kiss of love (1 Peter 5:14, *agape*). Whatever happened to the kind of love that David shared with Jonathan—passing the love of women?

We live in a day of cold, organized, church-building religion. We have Constantine to thank for that. Since the day that he made Christianity the state religion, the church of Jesus Christ hasn't been the same, until recently at least. There is a movement about today, reminiscent of the very early church, pre-Constantine. I welcome it. I welcome it with enthusiasm. The fires of love and individual worth are beginning to kindle again. And ironically, it's beginning with our children. Flower children, some of them were called. And still today, Jesus Freaks. "A little child shall lead them"? I guess that wasn't so dumb.

14

RIGHT AND WRONG

I would be the first to deny that the days in which we live are days of moral enlightenment. I'm not thrilled about the garbage on the newsstand or X-rated films. I don't see the value of drunkenness or sexual excess. I recognize that the Bible states that certain activities and attitudes are sinful. But I'm distressed about the Christian's concept of what is sin and what is not.

At one point there is no argument. If the Bible states that a given activity or attitude is sinful, then it is sinful. A Christian has no business engaging in anything that the Bible declares as wicked. He doesn't have to pray about it. He doesn't have to think it over. If the Scripture is clear on the matter, then it's settled.

But so many prohibitions among evangelical Christians are nowhere mentioned in the Bible and have served to help no one, in my opinion. Their stringency and the resultant boxed-in environment have driven believers into a shell, or into depression, anxiety, or even rejection of Christianity altogether. Many people stretch a point and try to tie a given prohibition with a Bible text that can be construed to imply such an application. This is very bad. It doesn't help; it damages.

In some cases, Christians are instructed that certain activities are wrong when the Word of God gives ample evidence for the *support* of such activities. In some circles, it is emphasized that the pastor is supposed to "do the work of an evangelist," the idea being that this is a primary function of his ministry. (After all, isn't this what Paul instructed Timothy to do?) But if someone in those same circles suggested that it might be all right if a present-day Christian took a glass of wine with his dinner, because Paul seemed to think it would be helpful for Timothy, the theological logic suddenly disappears. I have strongly agreed that if the Bible says something is wrong, then it is wrong. By the same token, if Scripture says or clearly implies that something is not wrong, then we're not helping matters or people when we say that it is!

Further, sometimes sin is relative. Sometimes it depends upon the "situation." Paul makes this clear in Romans 14 where he remarks, "Happy is he that condemneth not himself in that thing which he alloweth . . . for whatsoever is not of faith is sin." He goes on, "I know and am persuaded by the Lord Jesus, that there is nothing unclean of itself: but to him that esteemeth anything to be unclean, to him it is unclean." It is clear by this that when a person thinks he is sinning by participating in a certain activity, then he is indeed sinning. But for another to participate in the same activity may or may not be sin. It depends upon him and his own "persuaded mind" before God. One man's soup may well be another man's poison.

In this chapter Paul also discusses the matter of "offending" one's brother. He is talking about the brother who is *weak* in the faith, which is interesting. He isn't talking about these old Christian "salts" who are so set in their ways that nothing could shake them. He's speaking of someone who may follow another's example into an activity which (for him) might well cause him to *offend God* by sinning.

We cannot live our lives by the whims and dictates of another Christian's hangups. We cannot deny ourselves a Godgiven pleasure simply because Agatha Anguish down at the church might not approve. We need not live in fear and trepidation of what the pastor might think, or what Deacon Jones might say if he knew. These people, hopefully, are strong. The worst they could do would be to criticize you for enjoyment of something which to them is "wordly." But we must be concerned for the weak brother whose spiritual life is not so well established. If he does what we do, he might sin.

SOCIAL OR PEER GROUP CONSIDERATIONS

At the risk of sounding petty, I want to touch on how our lives as believers should be influenced by the likes and dislikes of those around us. Many people decide what they wear, eat, drink, and what activities they engage in, what to avoid, what they should do, etc., in accord with the image they want to project to others. They are concerned overmuch, in my opinion, with what others might think of them.

Trying to conform to the thinking and expectations of others has been a sore point for many ministers and their families. Long ago I decided that I would not make "superficial" demands of others. I would accept them and love them for whatever they were. I decided that I would conduct my life as though they felt the same way about me.

All of us must learn to be ourselves without apology. This isn't to say that we can run roughshod over the rights and feelings of others. But an individual must learn to respect himself for what he is in himself. He must never "look down" on himself. God has accepted him whatever his condition and a man must accept himself as well. He must be what Dwight Eisenhower called "his own man," within the perspective of God's viewpoint of him—which is high, not low.

THE CHRISTIAN AND "THE FLESH"

All believers, I am sure, are aware of the conflict that goes on in them, which Paul described in Romans 7:24. "O wretched man that I am! who shall deliver me from the body of this death?" All of us have felt this time and again. But some live in constant cognizance and morbid chagrin over how wicked they are. Their sin is always before them. The fact that Paul didn't constantly dwell on his own sinful condition is shown by his answering his own question. He thanks God for what he has done for him through Jesus Christ our Lord.

Paul knew that his old nature had been crucified with Christ. And he tells us in Romans 6 to "reckon ourselves to be dead indeed to sin [old sin nature], but alive to God through Jesus Christ." All of us are aware that our old nature is very much alive. Each day it makes its influence known. Paul's instruction to "reckon it to be dead" seems to me that he means for us to ignore it! Don't give it any thought. It doesn't deserve the time it takes to think about it. We have been washed—cleansed of all sin; we have been redeemed. As far as God is concerned, the old sin nature doesn't even exist. We need to view ourselves from God's viewpoint.

All believers sin. John tells us in his first epistle that we are liars if we don't admit that. But it's dangerous to mental and spiritual health to dwell upon it. We must not go about wringing our hands over our sins. God has accepted us. He has declared us to be as righteous as he is. Let us never willfully sin. But when we do, let us "agree to it" and continue on under the control of the Spirit of God.

THE DEVIL MADE ME DO IT

People give Satan credit for too much. He isn't that big of a deal. The way many Christians act toward Satan would make you think he's as big as God. Here are some of the things that Satan cannot do: He cannot know for certain what is in the mind of the believer. He cannot know with certainty the thoughts of the child of God. In other words, he can't read our minds. Testimony to this fact is seen in his wrong evaluation of Job. Satan thought Job would curse God to his face. *He was wrong.*

Oh, he's a master psychologist. He knows the patterns of human behavior better than anyone, and because of this he may influence behavior by arranging circumstances to formulate powerful temptation. *But he can't force a Christian to do anything.* As a matter of fact, believers are empowered by God to give Satan fits if they so desire. James tells us that if we give Satan a little resistance, he will *flee* from us (James 4:7). Remember, we believers have a unique advantage over Satan, an advantage unbelievers don't have: the presence of the Holy Spirit with whom we cohabit. So, that slogan is all wet; there's nothing the devil can *make* us do.

15

GOD'S WILL

One of the questions new believers most frequently ask is, "How can I know the will of God for my life?" Many inadequate and unfortunate answers to this inquiry have only served to cloud the issue. For some, who believe they are little more than puppets to be maneuvered as God pulls the strings, this matter has become a source of emotional conflict. Nor is the problem confined to those who have newly come to Christ. The issue of the will of God in the mind of the believer often lingers for many years; well-meaning people spend their lives searching for an elusive dream.

I believe that God is less central regarding the details of his "will" than many like to think. We must realize that God operates in accord with established rules which he himself brought into existence. The teleological argument for the existence of God tells us that God is a God of order, plan, and purpose more than it tells us anything else; it's only right, then, to assume that he accommodated the life experience of each believing Christian into his purpose. He has a purpose or plan or will for each of us, but it is to be understood within the framework of his established order.

As a part of this order, God has supplied men with intellect, emotion, and will. As a sovereign act, and intrinsic to the fundamental nature of his creation, God has provided man with the power to choose. Why are we forced by some to think that because one becomes a Christian, God relieves him of his function to make decisions for himself?

Throughout my Christian experience, I've been taught that God has a will for me and that my job is to find out what it is. *There is a whole system of Christian mentality which suggests that God's will is* necessarily *separate and distinct from my own.* The idea is that I must give up my own will in preference to God's. Because of this erroneous ideology, most believers are off on a "holy grail" type of search for the "will of God."

Here are some thoughts that may help us to realize an amazing fact: God wants us to "do our own thing"!

First, Psalm 37:4 seems to indicate that God will find pleasure in giving me what I want. God will give me the desires of my heart. Imagine that! If my delight is in Christ, then I can do what I want. So, if I really want to know the will of God, assuming I've met the first requirement, all I have to do is determine what I really want out of life and go after it. I can be assured that God is directing me.

Second, Jesus said, "My meat is to do the will of him that sent me" (John 4:34). The above point isn't meant to suggest that the will of the believer is necessarily the will of God. Experience often proves the contrary. But if I seriously desire to do his will, I have every reason to believe that God will bring my own desires into conformity with his. He will "give" my heart its desires. It's interesting that Jesus did this very thing. He *believed* that God was operating through him—and he was.

"For it is God that worketh in you both to will and to do of his good pleasure" (Philippians 2:13). This is the third major reason why believers shouldn't fret about God's will for their lives. If they have been regenerated by the Holy Spirit, he is operating within them to bring about his will and his pleasure. Nothing could be plainer than this.

There are limitations, obviously. If something is expressly forbidden in Scripture, or if God has already expressed his will, then obviously it isn't his will to go against it. But we dare not go to the extreme that is being popularized by some Christian men of influence: that "whenever a decision is to be made, determine what the 'natural' reaction would be, and then do the opposite. God's will is always contrary to our will." This is nonsense. The will of God is most likely to be the desire and will of the Christian who sincerely desires to do the will of God. So remember the formula: Delight yourself in the Lord and he will give you the *desires of your own heart.* This isn't to say that God hands us our whims on a silver platter. We must determine, in terms of specifics, exactly what we want from life or to do in life, believe that God has aided in the decision, and go after it. Work for it. Make plans and put them into effect.

This brings us to some final thoughts in connection with restructuring the mind of the believer. In the process of determining exactly what it is a believer desires in life, he should formulate it as a goal. Moreover, he very likely will want to do more than just one specific thing. In all probability, what he desires will require a number of intermediate steps before achieving it. Therefore, he should establish long-range or lifetime goals, intermediate goals, and short-range goals. These objectives should be real. They should represent his own personal desires. He needn't worry about the validity of his desires, if they don't conflict with the revealed will of God. Then he should determine to spend his life in their pursuit and achievement. This, in and of itself, is immensely rewarding and provides direction and purpose to life. The pursuit and struggle to reach an objective is often more satisfying than the objective itself.

I recall a story that I heard or read somewhere which illustrates this point. It seems a man in a small rural community purchased a plot of land. It had been poorly cared for and was filled with rocks, weeds, and assorted debris—in short, it was an eyesore. The new owner rolled up his sleeves and went to work. He removed the rocks, weeds, and debris. He plowed and cultivated the earth. He planted, enriched the soil with fertilizer, irrigated, and worked hard and long in his efforts to improve the property. In a few weeks he had nurtured a beautiful stand of corn and other vegetables. It was the pride of the community. A pious neighbor stopped by one day while he was hoeing and remarked, "My, the Lord has certainly given you a beautiful piece of land, my friend." The new owner stopped his labor in the blazing sun and replied, "Yes, indeed he has. But you should have seen it when the Lord had it all to himself!"

God has provided the natural resources. He has given us intellect, emotions, and the ability to determine. If we are to help people cope with life, we must help them to realize this.

PART IV

The
Medicine
Chest

16

THE PLACE
OF THE BIBLE

It was intimated earlier how a medical doctor is so thoroughly familiar with the medicines at his disposal that he can write prescriptions from memory. This is no small feat. As a high school student I worked in the neighborhood drugstore, and I became quite familiar with the prescription department. My employer was the owner-pharmacist, and he often let me fill certain simple prescriptions under his close supervision. I even learned to read the incredible scribblings most doctors use when writing prescriptions. I also was very impressed with the enormous number of different medicines on the store shelves, hundreds if not thousands.

I really don't know if each doctor has all these medicines memorized or not. I assume that he uses them often enough to be familiar with most of them. But it strikes me that ministers of the gospel, Christian counselors, and therapists, as well as Christian men and women, ought to be at least as familiar with the Bible as a doctor is with medicines. The Bible is our "medicine chest." The Word of God is our pharmaceutical storehouse from which we draw the appropriate "medicine" to treat human ills of the spirit and soul.

I don't hesitate to posit the Bible as the most effective therapeutic tool in the treatment of spiritual and mental ills that the world has ever known. Someone has said that the Bible isn't a scientific book, but where it touches upon science, it is scientifically accurate. I suppose this is a good dictum in most cases, but in the field of psychology and human behavior it most certainly is invalid. With regard to these fields, the Scripture is not only a book of science, it is *the* book of science. In addition to its purpose in revealing God, the Scripture serves as a basis and guide for human life and faith. It provides, as well, proven therapy for deviation from its guidelines.

Quite obviously, when I talk in terms of the Bible's being therapeutic, I am speaking primarily to people who possess the knowledge of Christ and have acted upon it. However, it would be a mistake to think that biblical truth and its application are ineffective for the nonbeliever. The principles of psychotherapy, which supposedly find their origin in experimentation of theory, are often biblical truth disguised in modern dress.

The Scripture passages in Part IV are essential to the knowledge of the therapist who wishes to be an effective counselor in the hand of God. I have chosen these passages from various translations of the Scripture because I feel they best represent the content and intent of the original.

THE TWENTY-THIRD PSALM

The Lord is my Shepherd; I shall not want. He maketh me to lie down in green pastures: he leadeth me beside the still waters. He restoreth my soul: he leadeth me in the paths of righteousness for his name's sake. Yea, though I walk through the valley of the shadow of death, I will fear no evil: for thou art with me; thy rod and thy staff they comfort me. Thou preparest a table before me in the presence of mine enemies: thou anointest my head with oil; my cup runneth over. Surely goodness and mercy shall follow me all the days of my life; and I will dwell in the house of the Lord forever.

The impact of the twenty-third psalm upon the tortured mind of almost anyone can hardly be overemphasized. It is possibly the single most potent mind-healing agent in all of the Word of God.

I can testify to a marked leap in my own spiritual maturing process by a unique exposure to this passage. Charles Allen, who wrote *God's Psychiatry,* was apparently the first to suggest this procedure. He suggested that a person go over each phrase of the twenty-third psalm in his thoughts five times a day for seven days. So each morning as I was shaving, I rehearsed the psalm in my mind. After breakfast I did it again, and again after lunch and dinner. Then slowly, meditating on each thought and sometimes each word, the twenty-third psalm "sang" me to sleep. Life went on as usual during the week and difficulties came as they do every week. Sometimes, as I thought about the psalm, my eyes would fill. I had never known such inner power and confidence of spirit as I experienced that week. And the effect of it has not left me. I know it so well it is like breathing. Whenever a thought comes along which challenges it, that thought is often overwhelmed by the power of that psalm. Certainly this isn't to say that I have lived in sort of a spiritual euphoria since that time, but I've found that when I fail or sin, I rarely mope about it. How can I when faced with the truth of the twenty-third psalm?

Allen says: "The twenty-third psalm is a pattern of thinking, and when a mind becomes saturated with it, a new way of thinking and a new life are the result. It contains only 118 words. One could memorize it in a short time. In fact, most of us already know it. But its power is not in memorizing the words, but rather in thinking the thoughts."[1]

The trick, of course, is in getting the patient or counselee to adopt this as a consistent procedure for an entire week. It reminds me of the "huff" with which Naaman made his exit from Elisha. He was of no "mind" to dip himself seven times in the muddy Jordan River. He even began to evade the procedure by choosing alternative courses. But his servant remarked, "What if the prophet had told you to do something difficult—wouldn't you have done it?" Naaman agreed and decided to try it, and of course was healed.

1. Charles L. Allen, *God's Psychiatry* (Fleming H. Revell Company, 1953), p. 15.

I know that it's hard for us to imagine that someone with a thought disorder could possibly do this. This is because we have concluded that "thought disorder" is a mechanical mental posture over which the subject has no control. But that this is not a valid conclusion is abundantly attested by the success of Reality Therapy in the treatment of "incurable" psychotic patients. (Reality Therapy is discussed in Chapter 3.)

I have often wished that I had facilities to conduct an experimental study of psychotic patients using half of them as a control group. I would employ the above procedure with half of them and allow the others traditional therapy. It would be fascinating to observe the effect that the twenty-third psalm would have on them. If the experiment was successful, think of the influence it might have on the traditional psychiatric applecart.

The twenty-third psalm, as I have implied, seems to be in a class by itself. But other passages of Scripture when properly applied will also bring about behavioral change in the life of an individual. The nature of this change, hopefully, is of course beneficial and therapeutic.

17

CHERAPEUTIC PASSAGES

(1) ASSURANCE OF GOD'S INTIMATE KNOWLEDGE AND LOVING CARE

Psalm 23 (see page 120)

Psalm 31:19, 20
Oh how great is thy goodness, which thou hast laid up for them that fear thee; which thou hast wrought for them that trust in thee before the sons of men! Thou shalt hide them in the secret of thy presence from the pride of man: thou shalt keep them secretly in a pavilion from the strife of tongues.

Psalm 34:17–19
The righteous cry, and the Lord heareth, and delivereth them out of all their troubles. The Lord is nigh unto them that are of a broken heart; and saveth such as be of a contrite spirit. Many are the afflictions of the righteous: but the Lord delivereth him out of them all.

Psalm 91:1, 2
He that dwelleth in the secret place of the Most High shall
abide under the shadow of the Almighty. I will say of the
Lord, He is my refuge and my fortress: my God; in him
will I trust.

Nahum 1:7
The Lord is good, a stronghold in the day of trouble; and
he knoweth them that trust in him.

1 Peter 5:7
Throw all your worries on him, for he cares [worries] for
you—TEV.

1 John 4:16b
God is love, and whoever lives in love lives in God and
God lives in him—TEV.

Jude 24
Now to him who is able to keep you from falling and to
present you before his glory without fault and with un-
speakable joy . . .—Phillips.

(2) COPING WITH EXTERNAL PRESSURES

The difficulties associated with life in a pressure-cooker society present an uphill battle for almost everyone. Learning to cope
with the difficulties and pressures of modern life is no small
task even for the stable, solid personality. In fact, many Christian people "crack" under the strain and the results are often
painful. For some reason they are ignorant of or have never been
able to profit from the relief valves that God has provided in
his Word.

The following passages of Scripture will, when utilized properly,
bring relief from pressure and ability to cope with the general issues
of life.

Joshua 1:9
Have I not commanded you? Be strong and courageous!
Do not tremble or be dismayed, for the Lord your God is
with you wherever you go—NASB.

Psalm 37:5
Commit thy way unto the Lord; trust also in him; and he shall bring it to pass.

Romans 8:28
And we know that God causes all things to work together for good to those who love God, to those who are called according to His purpose—NASB.

Romans 8:28 is one of the most quoted verses of Scripture. It is easy to understand why. It's important to note that it does not say that all things *are* good, but that all things work together for good. This distinction is important because it's possible that some think that this statement renders any activity as morally right. This certainly is not the case. But it does state that any activity, whether morally right or not, is used by God on behalf of both himself and the believer.

This concept is not without precedent in Scripture. God apparently often used pagan people and their values and activities to bring about his purposes. Abimelech was used by God to enlighten both Abraham and Isaac (Genesis 20:9, 14; 26:10). The prostitute Rahab was used by God even though she told a blatant lie about the whereabouts of the two spies; and God blessed her for it. Not only did she survive the siege of Jericho, but she became an ancestor of the Messiah. Pagan Nebuchadnezzar was a tool in the hands of God, and so was Cyrus the Great.

This verse and these considerations tell us more than anything else that nothing can befall a child of God that can contribute negatively to God's ultimate purpose for him. That is good news indeed.

2 Corinthians 4:7–10
This priceless treasure we hold, so to speak, in a common earthenware jar—to show that the splendid power of it belongs to God and not to us. We are handicapped on all sides, but we are never frustrated; we are puzzled, but never in despair. We are persecuted, but we never have to stand it alone: we may be knocked down but we are never knocked out! Every day we experience something of the

death of Jesus, so that we may also know the power of the life of Jesus in these bodies of ours—Phillips.

2 Corinthians 12:9
". . . My grace is all you need; for my power is strongest when you are weak." I am most happy, then, to be proud of any weaknesses, in order to feel the protection of Christ's power over me—TEV.

1 Peter 5:7 (see 1).

1 John 5:4, 5
. . . for every child of God is able to defeat the world. This is how we win the victory over the world: with our faith. Who can defeat the world? Only he who believes that Jesus is the Son of God—TEV.

(3) KNOWING THE WILL OF GOD

We have already discussed this matter to some extent. Here are some passages that provide pertinent information.

Psalm 37:4
Delight thyself also in the Lord; and he shall give thee the desires of thine heart.

Psalm 91:1, 2 (see 1.)

Proverbs 3:5, 6
Trust in the Lord with all thine heart; and lean not unto thine own understanding. In all thy ways acknowledge him, and he shall direct thy paths.

Proverbs 4:26
Watch the path of your feet, And all your ways will be established—NASB.

Romans 14:5b
Let every man be fully persuaded in his own mind.

Galatians 6:4
Each one should judge his own conduct for himself. If it is good, then he can be proud of what he himself has done, without having to compare it with what someone else has done—TEV.

Ephesians 5:15–17
So pay close attention to how you live. Don't live like
ignorant men, but like wise men. Make good use of every
opportunity you get, because these are bad days. Don't be
fools then, but try to find out what the Lord wants you to
do —TEV.

Philippians 2:13
For it is God which worketh in you both to will and to
do of his good pleasure.

Colossians 2:6
Just as you received Christ Jesus the Lord, so go on living
in him—in simple faith—Phillips.

(4) STABILITY IN LIFE

These passages represent truth that will mollify the anxieties
caused by feelings of insecurity. People who feel insecure need to
sink their roots into the commitments God has made to them about
the stability of their immediate and long-range future:

Joshua 1:8
This book of the Law shall not depart from your mouth,
but you shall meditate on it day and night, so that you may
be careful to do according to all that is written in it; for
then you will make your way prosperous, and then you
will have success—NASB.

Psalm 1:1–3
Blessed is the man that walketh not in the counsel of
the ungodly, nor standeth in the way of sinners, nor sit-
teth in the seat of the scornful. But his delight is in the
Law of the Lord; and in his law doth he meditate day
and night. And he shall be like a tree planted by the riv-
ers of water, that bringeth forth his fruit in his season; his
leaf also shall not wither; and whatsoever he doeth shall
prosper.

Psalm 37:3–7
Trust in the Lord, and do good; so shalt thou dwell in the
land, and verily thou shalt be fed. Delight thyself also in

the Lord; and he shall give thee the desires of thy heart. Commit thy way unto the Lord; trust also in him; and he shall bring it to pass. And he shall bring forth thy righteousness as the light, and thy judgment as the noonday. Rest in the Lord, and wait patiently for him: fret not thyself because of him who prospereth in his way, because of the man who bringeth wicked devices to pass.

Isaiah 40:31

Yet those who wait for the Lord will gain new strength; they will mount up with wings like eagles, they will run and not get tired, they will walk and not become weary— NASB.

Isaiah 41:10

Do not fear, for I am with you; do not anxiously look about you, for I am your God. I will strengthen you, surely I will help you, surely, I will uphold you with My righteous right hand—NASB.

Philippians 4:19

But my God shall supply all your need according to his riches in glory by Christ Jesus.

(5) INTERNAL PEACE

So many of us are distressed by inner turmoil. So many people desire inner peace of mind and spirit. But somehow it always seems to be just beyond reach. Many verses provide help for someone in this condition, but only three which seem to me the most meaningful are mentioned here:

John 14:27

I am leaving you with a gift—peace of mind and heart! And the peace I give isn't fragile like the peace the world gives. So don't be troubled or afraid—TLB.

Isaiah 26:3, 4

Thou wilt keep him in perfect peace, whose mind is stayed on thee: because he trusteth in thee. Trust ye in the Lord for ever: for in the Lord Jehovah is everlasting strength.

Philippians 4:6, 7
Don't worry about anything, but in all your prayers ask God for what you need, always asking him with a thankful heart. And God's peace, which is far beyond human understanding, will keep your hearts and minds safe, in Christ Jesus—TEV.

(6) PURPOSE, OBJECTIVES, AND DETERMINATION

One of the dearest men I have known, (and also one of the most maligned by others) made the remark, "No man can soar higher than he is able to think, by the grace of God." He also suggested as good advice for any Christian the statement: "I am determined not to be excelled." In spite of the "straw man" caricature which many people hold about Dr. Bob Jones, Sr., he was probably one of the most beloved and gracious men of his time. To me he was a curious mixture of Elijah and John, the beloved apostle. While he was living I was afraid to doubt that God would hurl down sheets of flame at his demand; and yet I was among the many who considered themselves one of his "little children." In the pulpit his words were fire and flowers, but on a one-to-one basis he was a deep and profound friend.

Whatever one may think about the stormy life of Bob Jones, Sr., he most certainly was a man of accomplishment. He often told us to get under the influence of a great idea. Determine to bring it to pass, and then by God's grace, spend the rest of your life bringing it to pass. That he followed his own advice is a matter of record. Obviously he was a great inspiration to me. Motivation, determination, and purpose are the special charisma and calling of the child of God. No one should be more motivated. Sadly, it turns out that many believers are just as bewildered and confused about purpose as they were before conversion. This feeling often prompts a conclusion of worthlessness and even suicide. These verses are offered as a therapeutic tool to combat this spiritual and mental disease:

Deuteronomy 8:18a
But thou shalt remember the Lord thy God: for it is he that giveth thee the power to get wealth . . .

Joshua 1:8 (see under 4)

Psalm 1:1–3 (see under 4)

1 Chronicles 4:10
And Jabez called on the God of Israel, saying, Oh that
thou wouldst bless me indeed, and enlarge my coast, and
that thine hand might be with me, and that thou wouldest
keep me from evil, that it may not grieve me! And God
granted him that which he requested.

Galatians 6:4 (see under 3)

Ephesians 5:15–17 (see under 3)

Philippians 3:13, 14
Brethren, I count not myself to have apprehended: but this
one thing I do, forgetting those things which are behind,
and reaching forth unto those things which are before, I
press toward the mark for the prize of the high calling of
God in Christ Jesus.

Ephesians 4:28b
... let him labor ... that he may have to give to him that
needeth.

Philippians 2:13 (see under 3)

Philippians 4:13
I can do all things through Christ which strengtheneth
me.

Philippians 4:19 (see under 4)

Psalm 84:11b
... no good thing will he withhold from them that walk
uprightly.

(7) FEAR OF DEATH

I have met many who desperately fear the horrible specter of
dying. But death is not an enemy to the child of God; it can be
considered a friend. Paul understood this when he wrote the following:

1 Corinthians 15:55
O death, where is thy sting? O grave, where is thy victory?

2 Corinthians 5:8
We are full of courage, and would much prefer to leave
our home in this body and be at home with the Lord—
TEV.

Philippians 1:21, 23
For to me to live is Christ, and to die is gain. . . . For I
am in a strait betwixt two, having a desire to depart, and
to be with Christ; which is far better.

(8) SPIRITUAL POWER

If one is a true Christian, one cannot escape the dynamic of the
indwelling presence of the Spirit of God. He is there, but the
posture or the attitude of his presence is of critical importance. The
Spirit must control the believer if his power or energy is to evidence
itself experientially. Christians in spiritual and mental difficulty are
rarely under the influence of the Spirit's controlling power. If they
are, his influence is only spasmodic and erratic. There is little
continuity or substance to their spiritual strength.

Belief is the determining factor. This, of course, is the case with
the acceptance of any scriptural truth. But a believer must believe
and trust firmly in the dynamic action of the indwelling Spirit, or
he is of little use.

I'm not sure I am fond of the well-known phrase, "Let go and
let God." It seems to suggest a passive role for the believer in his
relationship with the indwelling Spirit. It is my practice and conviction to use or manipulate the power of the Spirit of God. In my
mind it goes like this: The Spirit indwells us, and when he controls
us, his power is made available to us. We use that power as an act
of our own faith and determination, believing that God is guiding
our determination (Philippians 2:13). This dynamic, energy, or
whatever designation we give it, becomes active in every decision
and experience of life—and particularly in the cultivation of the
spiritual "gifts" spoken of earlier.

Acts 1:8a
. . . but you shall receive power when the Holy Spirit has
come upon you; and you shall be my witnesses. . . .
—NASB.

Note that this is a declarative statement, not a command. It's a statement of fact, not a statement of what believers should be. It has reference to Pentecost, where the baptism of all believers by the Holy Spirit took place. But the focus of our attention is upon the fact that the believer receives "power" when the Spirit has come. The believer possesses the power. It is not intrinsic power, native to the nature of the human. It is divine, supernatural power placed at the disposal of the human. He must use it.

Chaplain Merlin R. Carothers points out how he came to understand this truth in his little book *Prison to Praise*. He indicates that his desire was to be used by God. He wanted *God to use him.* He requested prayer with this in mind. His prayer was answered with the realization that God did not want to use him. Christ wanted the chaplain to *use him!* After this he remarks, "It was as if a door had opened into a new understanding of Jesus. He wants to give Himself for us each moment of our lives just as completely as He gave Himself on the cross."[1]

The power of God is there; it must be used:

> *Ephesians 1:16–19*
> I have not stopped giving thanks to God for you. I remember you in my prayers, and ask the God of our Lord Jesus Christ, the glorious Father, to give you the Spirit, who will make you wise and reveal God to you, so that you will know him. I ask that your minds may be open to see his light, so that you will know what is the hope to which he has called you, how rich are the wonderful blessings he promises his people, and how very great is his power at work in us who believe . . .—TEV.

> *Ephesians 3:16–20*
> I ask God, from the wealth of his glory, to give you power through his Spirit to be strong in your inner selves, and that Christ will make his home in your hearts, through faith. I pray that you may have your roots and foundations in love, and that you, together with all God's people, may have the power to understand how broad and long and

---

1. Merlin R. Carothers, *Prison to Praise* (Plainfield, New Jersey, Logos International, 1970), p. 48.

high and deep is Christ's love. Yes, may you come to know
his love—although it can never be fully known—and so be
completely filled with the perfect fullness of God—TEV.

(9) DESTINY CONTROLLED BY GOD

It is true. The sovereign God controls our lives. It may be
paradoxical that we are to use the power of God and all the while
he is the One who is manipulating us, but it is true. This, of course,
is of no small comfort and importance to the believer who has
committed his welfare to God. A believer who does not have a deep
sense of God's control of things, and is not aware that his is a
beneficial control, is prone to anxiety, even to thought disorder.
Verses that can help in such cases are:

Romans 8:28 (see 2)

Ephesians 1:11
. . . also we have obtained an inheritance, having been
predestined according to His purpose who works all
things after the counsel of His will—NASB.

Philippians 2:13 (see under 3)

1 John 5:4, 5 (see under 2)

(10) THE CERTAINTY OF ETERNAL LIFE

I have lost count of the people I know who, because of an
irregularity in spiritual experience, believe that God no longer
loves them and that they no longer possess eternal life. I do not
mean here to fly in the face of my Arminian friends. It has been
my experience with the so-called Calvinistic and Arminian schools
of theology that, by and large, both believe the same thing but say
it in different ways. I've never met a responsible, well-taught Christian and well-adjusted personality of the Arminian background
who wasn't assured beyond any doubt that he would go to heaven
when he died. On the other hand, I've met many Calvinist Christians who were afraid they were lost. I sometimes wonder how
Calvin and Arminius would respond if they knew of the contro-
versy they allegedly began. The passages below are just as well

known to the Arminian theologian as to a Calvinist. Both agree that a believer who is frightened about the prospect of not going to heaven has a problem. In some cases, it has been incapacitating.

Romans 8:29, 30
For whom he foreknew, he also did predestinate to be conformed to the image of his Son, that he might be the firstborn among many brethren. Moreover whom he did predestinate, them he also called: and whom he called he also justified: and whom he justified, them he also glorified.

Ephesians 1:3–6
Blessed be the God and Father of our Lord Jesus Christ, who has blessed us with every spiritual blessing in the heavenly places in Christ, just as He chose us in Him before the foundation of the world, that we should be holy and blameless before Him. In love He predestined us to adoption as sons through Jesus Christ to Himself, according to the kind intention of His will, to the praise of the glory of His grace, which He freely bestowed on us in the Beloved—NASB.

Ephesians 1:13, 14
In Him, you also, after listening to the message of truth, the gospel of your salvation—having also believed, you were sealed in Him with the Holy Spirit of promise, who is given as a pledge of our inheritance, with a view to the redemption of God's own possession, to the praise of his glory—NASB.

Ephesians 2:6, 7
And hath raised us up together, and made us sit together in heavenly places in Christ Jesus: That in the ages to come he might show the exceeding riches of his grace, in his kindness toward us, through Christ Jesus.

Philippians 1:6
For I am confident of this very thing, that He who began a good work in you will perfect it until the day of Christ Jesus—NASB.

1 Thessalonians 4:13–18

But we do not want you to be uninformed, brethren, about those who are asleep, that you may not grieve as do the rest who have no hope. For if we believe that Jesus died and rose again, even so God will bring with Him those who have fallen asleep in Jesus. For this we say to you by the word of the Lord, that we who are alive, and remain until the coming of the Lord, shall not precede those who have fallen asleep. For the Lord Himself will from heaven descend with a shout, with the voice of the archangel, and with the trumpet of God; and the dead in Christ shall rise first. Then we who are alive and remain shall be caught up together with them in the clouds to meet the Lord in the air, and thus we shall always be with the Lord. Therefore comfort one another with these words—NASB.

2 Thessalonians 2:14

And it was for this He called you through our gospel, that you may gain the glory of our Lord Jesus Christ—NASB.

1 John 3:1, 2

Behold, what manner of love the Father hath bestowed upon us, that we should be called the sons of God: therefore the world knoweth us not, because it knew him not. Beloved, now are we the sons of God, and it doth not yet appear what we shall be: but we know that, when he shall appear, we shall be like him; for we shall see him as he is.

(11) CHRISTIAN REWARD

I call them Christian "comic books." I view them with an unsympathetic eye. I have reference to those cartoon-like pamphlets which picture all the horrors attending anyone who does not properly believe in Christ. One to which I particularly object is the one depicting the believer having all his sordid sins flashed on a giant screen in heaven before the Judgment Seat of Christ and before all the eager eyes of his fellow believers. What a travesty! Minds that conceive such derangement of biblical fact are in severe need of help themselves. I am not being very loving, I know. I don't want to attack *people*—only their wrong concepts and the theological garbage they produce.

It is this kind of thinking that makes people afraid of God—if, in fact, they really believe it. God doesn't want anyone to be frightened of him any more than I want my kids or anyone else to be frightened of me. A cursory study of what takes place at the Judgment Seat of Christ will provide ample ammunition for this view—and this is precisely the point. That concept of God cannot possibly be the result of careful study of all that the Scripture has to say about the subject. In fact, it directly contradicts many of the passages.

The Judgment Seat of Christ is nothing to fear. It is something to anticipate joyfully. Its sole purpose concerns the dispensing of reward for service rendered by the child of God.

> *Ephesians 6:8*
> Knowing that whatsoever good thing any man doeth, the same shall he receive of the Lord . . .

> *2 Thessalonians 2:14 (see 10)*

> *2 Timothy 4:8*
> Henceforth there is laid up for me a crown of righteousness, which the Lord, the righteous judge, shall give me at that day: and not to me only, but unto all them also that love his appearing.

> *1 John 3:1, 2 (see 10)*

> *Jude 24 (see 1)*

> *Ephesians 5:27*
> That he might present it [the Church] to himself a glorious church, not having spot, or wrinkle, or any such thing; but that it should be holy and without blemish.

Any passage that seems to support the idea of exposure of sin in heaven must be taken in the light of the above passages. Let us note some of them:

> *1 Corinthians 3:11–15*
> For other foundation can no man lay than that is laid, which is Jesus Christ. Now if any man build upon this foundation gold, silver, precious stones, wood, hay, every

man's stubble work shall be made manifest: for the day shall declare it, because it shall be revealed by fire: and the fire shall try every man's work of what sort it is. If any man's work abide which he hath built thereupon, he shall receive a reward. If any man's work shall be burned, he shall suffer loss: but he himself shall be saved; yet so as by fire.

Keep in mind that the believer is not being tried in the scene this passage describes, but rather his works are being evaluated. The believer has already been tried and acquitted in Christ. He has the righteousness of Christ. *The believer is as righteous as the One before whom he stands at the Judgment Seat of Christ.*

The believer's works are made subject to the "fire." In what sense is this fire to be taken? The various works in this passage are described in the form of simile. That leads us to believe that the fire which is to try those works is a simile. In the same sense that the gold or wood are not real but only representative, the fire is not real but only representative. Representative of what? This fire must represent the evaluation of Jesus, the righteous Judge, of the quality of the believer's service. His evaluation of that quality will determine the nature of the believer's reward. The "loss" the believer "suffers" will be whatever effort he has spent in the service of Christ that did not contribute to his reward. The word *suffer* is better rendered *experience;* the believer will experience loss in the sense that his reward will be influenced negatively by unfaithful or hypocritical service. It does not refer to a "sense of loss." When Paul penned 2 Timothy 4:8 where he included everyone, he did not seem to make provision for a sense of loss. His viewpoint of the Judgment Seat of Christ was bright, hopeful, and eager.

2 Corinthians 5:9, 10 and Romans 14:10–12 must be viewed in the same perspective. I once talked with a minister who said that he has a "sense of accountability to God," taking his cue from Romans 14:12. I think my friend was right in his feeling, but that sense of accountability must bear further qualification. If he fears reprisal from God because of the failures in his life, or because of his sins, then his accountability is misconstrued. I have a sense of accountability to my wife. I must be faithful to her. I feel this way, not because of any legal or moral restrictions placed upon me, or

that I fear reprisal. I feel this way because *I love her* and because we have committed ourselves to each other. I have a sense of accountability to God, too, but it is an accountability of love, an accountability of mutual commitment.

(12) FORGIVENESS AND GUILT

The believer in Jesus Christ has had all his guilt atoned for. He is no longer guilty. Even the penalty for his former guilt has been paid. He has vicariously been totally and perfectly rehabilitated. He is not guilty. Therefore, the believer has no basis for feelings of guilt for any sin against God or others. This isn't to say that he won't have feelings of regret or sorrow. Paul calls this "godly sorrow which worketh repentance." In other words, if a sinful act has hurt or injured the feelings of others or of God, then the offender has violated the commitment of love, and this brings hurt to everyone concerned. For the believer to exist in a continuing state of guilt feelings is just as sinful and damaging as if he were insensitive to love.

> *Psalm 32:1, 2*
> Blessed is he whose transgression is forgiven, whose sin is covered. Blessed is the man unto whom the Lord imputeth not iniquity, and in whose spirit there is no guile.

> *Romans 8:1*
> There is therefore now no condemnation for those who are in Christ Jesus—NASB.

> *2 Corinthians 5:21*
> For he hath made him to be sin for us, who knew no sin; that we might be made the righteousness of God in him.

> *Ephesians 1:7*
> In Him we have redemption through His blood, the forgiveness of our trespasses, according to the riches of His grace—NASB.

> *Colossians 2:9–17*
> For in Him all the fulness of Deity dwells in bodily form, and in Him you have been made complete, and He is the head over all rule and authority; and in Him you were also circumcised with a circumcision made without hands, in

the removal of the body of the flesh by the circumcision of Christ: having been buried with Him in baptism, in which you were also raised up with Him through faith in the working of God, who raised Him from the dead. And when you were dead in your transgressions and the uncircumcision of your flesh, He made you alive together with Him, having forgiven us all our transgressions, having cancelled out the certificate of debt consisting of decrees against us and which was hostile to us; and He has taken it out of the way, having nailed it to the cross. When He had disarmed the rulers and authorities, He made a public display of them, having triumphed over them through Him. Therefore let no one act as your judge in regard to food or drink or in respect to a festival or a new moon or a Sabbath day—things which are a mere shadow of what is to come; but the substance belongs to Christ—NASB.

Titus 3:5
He saved us, not on the basis of deeds which we have done in righteousness, but according to His mercy, by the washing of regeneration and renewing by the Holy Spirit—NASB.

(13) MENTAL PROGRAMMING

It is possible for a person deliberately to construct a healthy, responsive mind. Very much could be said here for the process of mind development, in the sense of "positive achievement" mental attitude. The books written by Peale, Carnegie, Maltz, and Napoleon Hill suggested in the bibliography are of vital assistance in this regard. Many people "pooh-pooh" this sort of thing, but the fact remains—it works! Any psychologist will tell you that the mind can be trained to respond to given stimuli and circumstances in a predictable manner. Any reasonable goal can be accomplished by sheer mental determination regardless of "natural" ability. Countless examples demonstrate this. The Apostle Paul knew it:

Philippians 4:8
Finally, brethren, whatever is true, whatever is honorable, whatever is right, whatever is pure, whatever is lovely,

whatever is of good repute, if there is any excellence and
if anything worthy of praise, let your mind dwell on these
things—NASB.

Philippians 4:13 (see under 6)

Peter also was cognizant of this phenomenon:

2 Peter 1:5–8
Now for this very reason also, applying all diligence, in
your faith supply moral excellence, and in your moral
excellence, knowledge; and in your knowledge, self-control, and in your self-control, perseverance, and in your
perseverance, godliness; and in your godliness, brotherly
kindness, and in your brotherly kindness, Christian love.
For if these qualities are yours and are increasing, they
render you neither useless nor unfruitful in the true
knowledge of our Lord Jesus Christ—NASB.

(14) STRENGTH OF CONSCIENCE (FAITH)

In order to be mentally healthy, a believer must have confidence
in the validity of his own thoughts. He must not constantly fret
over whether or not an idea he has comes from God, or the lust
of the flesh, or the devil. In other words, he must have confidence
in his own conscience:

Proverbs 16:3
Commit thy works unto the Lord, and thy thoughts shall
be established.

If a man will commit his actions to the Lord (that is, whatever
he does is done either consciously or unconsciously with divine
values in view—which includes such things as recreation, pleasure,
work, human relationships, etc.), the Scripture indicates that God
will direct (establish) his thoughts. He may have confidence that
his will reflects that of God himself.

1 John 3:20–22
For if our heart condemn us, *God is greater than our heart*
[Italics mine; the implication here is that we are wrong in
allowing our heart to condemn us, and that God overrules

such condemnation], and knoweth all things. Beloved, if our heart condemn us not, then have we confidence toward God. And whatsoever we ask, we receive of him, because we keep his commandments, and do those things that are pleasing in his sight.

In answer to the question "What are his commandments?" the answer is twofold:

1 John 3:23
And this is his commandment, That we should [1] believe on the name of his Son Jesus Christ, and [2] love one another, as he gave us commandment.

These two commandments comprise all the "rules" for Christian living. They are the standard by which all other imperatives are measured. They are the standard by which we are measured.

(15) OBLIGATORY COMMANDS TO THE BELIEVER

I am genuinely concerned about the rigidity that most Christians impose upon themselves, thinking they are somehow pleasing God. Personally, I think legalism has done infinitely more harm to the Body of Christ than the worst forms of license. I need not go into the list of do's and don'ts that most Christians consider to be "God's standards," but they are legion. It is this very problem that has driven believers to the therapist's office. In my opinion, self-imposed legalism is the single greatest cause for guilt complexes, anxieties, and general unhappiness with life.

The real negatives of Christian living can be grouped into three areas:

(1) *Those things that the Bible specifically declares to be wrong are sinful.* It is interesting how many believers are very strong about some of these items and ignore others. It is interesting also how some violently denounce "borderline" or nonexistent sins, while openly participating in some of the specified negatives of the Bible. Sins of omission (James 4:17) are included in this category.

(2) *We have sinned if we have caused someone else to sin.* This is the result of a deliberate act. It requires at least two things in my judgment: (a) knowledge that what we are doing, saying, etc., will cause someone else to sin; and, (b) awareness by the other person that we are engaged in the activity which if he did, he would be sinning.

(3) *Those things that are sinful because the believer thinks them to be sinful.* However, 1 John 3:20–22 may have some mediating influence upon this in certain situations.

But Christian living is not made up of conformity to objective "standards." It is made up of an expression of love in the life of God.

Micah 6:8
He hath showed thee, O man, what is good; and what doth the Lord require of thee, but to do justly, and to love mercy, and to walk humbly with thy God?

John 13:34, 35
A new commandment I give to you, that you love one another, even as I have loved you, that you also love one another. By this all men will know that you are My disciples, if you have love one for another—NASB.

1 John 3:23
And this is his commandment, that we should believe on the name of his Son Jesus Christ, and love one another, as he gave us commandment.

Romans 13:9, 10
The commandments, "Do not commit adultery; do not murder; do not steal; do not covet,"—all these, and any others besides, are summed up in the one command, "Love your neighbor as yourself." Whoever loves his neighbor will never do him wrong. To love, is to obey the whole Law—TEV.

Galatians 5:13
For brethren, we have been called unto liberty; only use not liberty for an occasion to the flesh, but by love serve one another.

(16) MARITAL PROBLEMS

So much Scripture could be cited at this point. In every single marital problem I have had experience with, it has been the result of lack of conformity to God's family plan. There have been no exceptions. It seems to me that the focal point of all marital problems stems from the cooling of love on the part of one or both partners. The most therapeutic passage in all of the Word of God for the healing of marital difficulties is also probably the most neglected—and if not the most neglected, the most abused. I refer to the Song of Solomon.

What the vast majority of fine theologians have done with this precious and exquisite portion of the Bible borders on the unforgivable. Men have allegorized, spiritualized, and symbolized this poor passage of Scripture so extensively that one must wade through piles of commentary to find one single writer who will be honest in his interpretation. This is a subject upon which I could write many words of lament. Propriety restrains me. I simply want to say that there is no basis whatsoever for surmising the Song of Solomon to be anything else but God's viewpoint of conjugal love. It is sensual. It is erotic. It is beautiful beyond description. If it can be applied in all of its expression of marital love and in the most generous manner possible, it will work miracles for a tense marriage.

I am not simply theorizing here, I speak both from personal experience with my own marriage, and from counseling situations. At one point I gave a comprehensive series of messages on the Song to my congregation, in which I drew no "punches" nor did I water down any of the more graphic descriptions. I was very fearful of doing this. Victorian influences are strong among believers, even in southern California. It was not without a great deal of trepidation that I entered into this arena. But I felt compelled by God to enter it, and I did. I am still amazed at the response. There was not a single word of criticism. I did receive some good-natured ribbing about my X-rated sermons. But words of appreciation were kind and profuse. More important, the effect among the families was similarly rewarding.

I have consulted many translations of the Song of Solomon, in addition to linguistic critical analyses. I have found no translation that equals that of the *New English Bible* both in beauty and in adherence to the intent of the original language. I commend it to your use.

Beginning with the Song of Solomon, the therapist may want to broaden the understanding of love by a careful comprehension of 1 Corinthians 13, and beyond that to intramarital relationships as suggested in Ephesians 5:21–32 and Colossians 3:18, 19. These are the basic passages in the Bible dealing with marriage as a whole. I have never had occasion to go beyond these.

(17) PARENT-CHILD PROBLEMS

Proverbs 6:20–23
My son, keep thy father's commandment, and forsake not the law of thy mother: Bind them continually upon thine heart, and tie them about thy neck. When thou goest, it shall lead thee; when thou sleepest, it shall keep thee; and when thou awakest, it shall talk with thee. For the commandment is a lamp; and the law is light; and reproofs of instruction are the way of life.

I must dissent from those who advance the book of Proverbs as the focus for guidance in the establishment of family relationships —that is, unless one wants to raise his children to be little Hebrews of the Solomonic age. It's true that Proverbs suggests many practical helps in all human relationships. Still, I caution parents about formulating their Christian family doctrine from the book of Proverbs. It is the wisdom of Solomon couched in proverbial form and it carries with it the same liability inherent in the book of Ecclesiastes. That is, it may represent as often as the wisdom of God, the conclusions of a man based upon his interpretation of observable phenomena. Even as I write this, I can hear the roars of those who are going to conclude that my doctrine of inspiration is awry. Let me assure those dear contentious souls that I believe the Bible is inspired, all sixty-six books. But I also suggest that the person who builds his family upon the book of Proverbs may let himself in for a lot of grief.

The above passage encapsulates the entire instruction of Proverbs on the subject of family relationships.

Ephesians 6:1–3
Children obey your parents in the Lord, for this is right. Honor your father and mother (which is the first commandment with a promise), That it may be well with you, and that you may live long on the earth—NASB.

Ephesians 6:4
And, fathers, do not provoke your children to anger; but bring them up in the discipline and instruction of the Lord —NASB.

Colossians 3:20, 21
Children, be obedient to your parents in all things, for this is well pleasing to the Lord. Fathers, do not exasperate your children, that they may not lose heart—NASB.

These are the critical passages. By and large, if they are accepted, harmony between parent and child will follow.

(18) CHRISTIAN LIBERTY

This has already been alluded to in our remarks about Christian rigidity. The following passages should help the believer realize that he is free to do what he wants in life, provided, of course, he does not overtly or covertly sin, and does not infringe upon the liberty of others. In a society of individuals, no single person is free to force himself upon another or to inhibit the freedom of another. Because of their length, some passages are only referred to:

John 8:32, 36
And you shall know the truth, and the truth shall make you free. . . . If therefore the Son shall make you free, you shall be free indeed—NASB.

Romans 6:6, 7; 17–22
Let us never forget that our old selves died with him on the cross that the tyranny of sin over us might be broken —for a dead man can safely be said to be immune to the power of sin. And if we were dead men with him we can

believe that we shall also be men newly alive with him.

Then, released from the service of sin, you entered the service of righteousness. (I use an everyday illustration because human nature grasps truth more readily that way.) In the past you voluntarily gave your bodies to the service of vice and wickedness—for the purpose of becoming wicked. So, now, give yourselves to the service of righteousness—for the purpose of becoming really good. For when you were employed by sin you owed no duty to righteousness . . . but now that you are employed by God, you owe no duty to sin, and you reap the fruit of being made righteous, while at the end of the road there is life for evermore—Phillips.

Romans 7:6
But now we have been released from the Law, having died to that by which we were bound, so that we serve in newness of the Spirit and not in oldness of the letter—NASB.

Romans 8:2
For the law of the Spirit of life in Christ Jesus has set you free from the law of sin and death.

Romans 14:1–23—NASB

1 Corinthians 8:1–13

Galatians 2:21
I do not frustrate the grace of God: for if righteousness come by the law, then Christ is dead in vain.

Galatians 5:1
Stand fast therefore in the liberty wherewith Christ hath made us free, and be not entangled again with the yoke of bondage.

Galatians 5:13, 14 (see 15)

Colossians 2:9–17 (see 12)

1 Timothy 4:4
For everything created by God is good, and nothing is to be rejected, if it is received with gratitude—NASB.

(19) SPIRITUAL GIFTS

These passages have been cited before. I cite them here for convenient reference:

Romans 12:6–8

1 Corinthians 12–14

Ephesians 4:11, 12

1 Peter 4:9–11

(20) POWER OVER SATANIC INFLUENCE

The believer must understand that Satan has no mystical power over him. Just the reverse is true. Satan cannot read the mind or know the thoughts of a believer in Christ.

James 4:7b
. . . Resist the devil and he will flee from you—NASB.

Job 1 ff.
(Satan was wrong in his assessment of Job's character and thoughts.)

Matthew 4 ff.
(Satan was wrong in his assessment of the character and thoughts of Jesus.)

1 John 4:4b
. . . greater is He who is in you than he who is in the world —NASB.

(21) SELF-IMAGE

Many believers have a poor self-image. They think themselves to be inadequate, miserable, worm-like creatures in whom God has only a passing interest. As suggested before, a believer would do well to view himself through the eyes of a loving and compassionate God:

Psalm 139:14–16
I will praise thee; for I am fearfully and wonderfully made:

marvelous are thy works, and that my soul knoweth right
well. My substance was not hid from thee when I was
made in secret, and curiously wrought in the lower parts
of the earth. Thine eyes did see my substance, yet being
unperfect; and in thy book all my members were written,
which in continuance were fashioned, when as yet there
was none of them.

(22) BALANCED, WELL-ADJUSTED
CHRISTIAN LIVING

To produce the qualities of the following passage is the goal of
every Christian therapist. It is the picture of the kind of Christian
that all of us should be:

Romans 12:9–21
Let love be without hypocrisy. Abhor what is evil; cleave
to what is good. Be devoted to one another in brotherly
love; give preference to one another in honor; not lagging
behind in diligence, fervent in spirit, serving the Lord;
rejoicing in hope, persevering in tribulation, devoted to
prayer, contributing to the needs of the saints, practicing
hospitality. Bless those who persecute you; bless and curse
not. Rejoice with those who rejoice, and weep with those
who weep. Be of the same mind toward one another; do
not be haughty in mind, but associate with the lowly. Do
not be wise in your own estimation. Never pay back evil
for evil to anyone. Respect what is right in the sight of all
men. If possible, so far as it depends on you, be at peace
with all men. Never take your own revenge, beloved, but
leave room for the wrath of God, for it is written, "Ven-
geance is mine, I will repay, says the Lord." But if your
enemy is hungry, feed him, and if he is thirsty, give him
a drink; for in doing so you will heap burning coals upon
his head. Do not be overcome by evil, but overcome evil
with good—NASB.

The passages of Scripture offered in this chapter are by no means
exhaustive. They are intended simply to form a basis for reference

and to form a foundation upon which a competent Christian therapist may construct additional therapeutic passages. It is hoped by
this writer that the reader will allow the twenty-third psalm to be
the backbone of his counseling ammunition, and that Song of
Solomon will be its flesh.

Therapeutic Technique

A: THE "HOW TO" OF LOVE THERAPY

Parts III and IV have indicated the basis and direction of Christian thought which I believe is correct and which should influence therapy. Chapters 2–4 dealt with the philosophical concepts upon which a sound therapeutic technique can be erected. Part A of the Appendix details the "how to" of Love (paracaletic) Therapy.

INVOLVEMENT AND PROPER DIAGNOSIS

Involvement and diagnosis are taken together because both represent a starting place in therapy. Diagnosis is really the place to begin, but the diagnostic process is incorporated into the establishment of involvement. In most cases (unless the problem is of an extremely minor nature, such as the clarification of the issues involved in a counselee decision—"minor" in the sense of the amount of time necessary to reach a solution), it is best to permit the first session of forty to fifty minutes to be a "get acquainted" session. At this time the patient articulates his problem as best he can. The therapist can offer any measures of relief that may temporarily suffice. The main thrust of this hour is orientation. An attempt at friendship should be extended. The therapist at this time can inform the counselee about certain methodologies he may want to use, such as tests, about psychoanalysis as detailed in this work, and about the mechanics of paracaletic therapy. But for the most part, the therapist indicates that he wants to become involved in the patient's life, insofar as office visits (or whatever the context of counseling) will permit.

In determining what is wrong with a patient, avoid labeling him as much as possible. Don't think of him in psychological terms. He is a person just like you. The therapist is no better or worse than the counselee. In the sight of God you are on the same level. The counselee must be made to feel that the therapist has no right to offer judgments or condemnatory allegations because he himself is guilty of the "same things." "Same things" is taken generically, not specifically. This feeling on the part of the counselee is a prerequisite to involvement. It tells the patient that the therapist is not an invulnerable paragon of Christian virtue. People who give this "image" to others are being gross in their hypocrisy. Almost anyone can see through it.

Answering the question "How do I become involved?" is not easy. Glasser indicates that it is a matter of becoming important and influential in the viewpoint of the patient. But I think it goes much deeper than this in the Christian context. Glasser is right in assuming that influence is necessary before guidance will be accepted, and he points out as well that the influence must be friendly, not ostentatious or officious. Still, this does not say it all. A Christian therapist must communicate love as well.

Love must not simply be expressed, it must be communicated. Communication does not take place just because there is a sender and a receiver. The sender must be sending, and the receiver must be receiving. If the latter of these two conditions is not true, if the receiver is not receiving what the sender is sending, then with respect to Christian love, the sender (therapist) must adjust conditions of his "signal" to the "frequency level" of the receiver. The receiver is too weak to make his own adjustment. A breakdown of communication often takes place in the church because a pastor loves his people, and yet his people are somehow not getting the message. So he turns up his volume. They still are not tuned in. *It is incumbent upon the* lover *to make the beloved* feel *loved by adjusting the expression of love to the point where it will find response.* This is an axiom of love which the therapist must understand and practice if he is going to become effectively and therapeutically involved with his patient. Unless love is felt by the recipient, it has not been communicated.

This communication may or may not take place at the initial contact with a patient. The chances are that it will develop in time. The emotional climate of the Christian therapist must be one of love, before any significant progress in involvement can be made.

Vulnerability is another important part of involvement. It is a wise practice for a therapist of the paracaletic school to share some of his own weaknesses with the patient. He must build the concept with the patient that he has something to offer to the therapist's life and experience as well. The idea that "we are in this thing together, we will bear one another's burdens, and together we will conquer it" is a framework in which involvement is nourished.

Charisma of confidence and stability should be projected as a genuine feature of a paracaletic therapist. Confidence upon which the counselee may come to depend is necessary. The counselee does not have confidence in himself and probably not in God either. He must have someone concrete with whom he can develop an appropriate and empathetic relationship. At a later point in therapy, it is an easy matter to transfer the dependency of the counselee from the therapist to God by simply demonstrating that the therapist himself is dependent upon God for his own strength.

A final element in establishing involvement is the demonstration of keen interest in the counselee's viewpoint and the acceptance of his identity as a good person. The paracaletic therapist and the environment for counseling must have a "Joe's Bar" type of atmosphere. The patron of "Joe's" knows that he can go there, wear anything he wants, say anything he wants, relax, be cool, tell his problems to Joe—and nobody will put him down for it.

How long it takes to become involved depends upon the severity of the patient's problem and the sincerity and ability of the therapist to become involved. But once it is achieved, there is hardly any request or instruction the therapist may make, that the patient will not try very hard to do. After all, he has someone who is with him and really trying to help him. When involvement is achieved, the therapist has discovered what the psychiatric community calls an "entry point," a place where therapy can be extended and will be received.

DEVELOPMENT OF RESPONSIBILITY

Development of responsibility comprises the final two steps of paracaletic therapy: (1) Developing the ability to distinguish between responsibility and irresponsibility, and (2) Developing the qualities of responsibility while rejecting the qualities of irresponsibility. The latter of these two represents the quotient of personality change.

(1)Developing the ability to distinguish between responsibility and irresponsibility:

The therapist must determine on what level of responsibility the patient is actuating. This determination depends almost entirely upon correct diagnosis. The therapist must determine as best he can exactly how far afield the patient is from the proper mental structure of spiritual normalcy. This chart will be helpful in this regard:

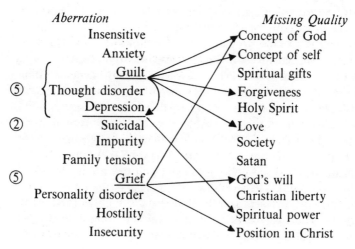

Arrows are drawn from the *problem* (underlined) of a particular patient to the respective spiritual inadequacy. This helps the therapist to know where the emphasis of his therapy will lie, as well as its nature. On a scale of 1–5, the therapist indicates his evaluation of the intensity of the various problems as a further guideline for the concentration of his efforts.

The arrows and other markings on the above example represent the case of Louis. Louis was a Marine recruit at a nearby camp, who was threatening to commit suicide. When I talked with him I discovered that he and his friend had enlisted together and that his friend had been accidentally killed by a truck on the base. Louis was convinced it was a suicide. His friend had been extremely despondent and had blamed Louis for persuading him to join. Louis, too, was reacting to the rigors of basic training. But his grief was real, and he now felt guilty and was extremely depressed because he thought he had contributed to his friend's death. The arrows represent the inadequacies of Louis's life and his severe lack of proper relationship to God. I felt that the threats of suicide were shallow and insincere, thus the indication of 2 in scale of intensity. In therapy, the threats were not even discussed. They were symptomatic of his grief, guilt, and depression, which registered 5 on my intensity evaluation.

I was able to achieve early involvement with Louis and had the privilege of bringing him to Christ. Two years later, I was honored to marry him to a lovely bride. He went on to Vietnam, where he earned the bronze star for bravery in action.

When the patient's present "level of responsibility" (Chapter 4) is discovered, he must be made to understand right concepts. This is done by instruction about the related precepts of Christian living, with specific attention given to the patient's weak areas. It is here that the paracaletic therapist must reach into his "medicine chest" (Part IV, Chapters 16, 17). As has already been suggested, those chapters form a good basic resource for specific Scriptures applicable to specific problems. Let me emphasize, too, that *how* scriptural truth is presented and explained is just as important as the use of the correct passages themselves.

Perhaps it's a bad idea to refer to the Bible as "medicine," or to suggest that all one needs to do is give the patient an applicable verse of Scripture ("a pill"). It doesn't work that way. Often people resent being "quoted" at. I can't say that I blame them. Also, many Christians believe that anything other than verbatim quotation is second-best, perhaps even an adulteration. It might be well to remind believers that unless they are able to quote Greek, it is impossible to recite Scripture verbatim. Indeed, Greek or not, no living human can quote the original Autographs. There is no mystical, sacred charisma to any translation. I believe in the plenary, verbal inspiration of the Scripture as much as anyone. But I am not afraid to present Bible truth in my own words and phraseology, doing my best to be faithful to the written text.

What I have to share of what God has given me originates with him, but it comes through me—all of me: intellect, emotions, and will. This is the process, incidentally, by which we received the Bible in the first place.

With this in mind, I want to suggest that the paracaletic therapist present the Scripture experientially. That is, that the truth is a part of him as well as in print on paper. Subtle suggestion based upon truth is more effective than parroting truth.

In some cases, however, it is advisable to suggest that a patient study a specific passage pertinent to his problem. Especially is this true with respect to the twenty-third psalm. I strongly endorse the procedure of meditation suggested by Dr. Charles Allen (Chapter 16). But generally speaking, it is better to see truth incarnated in the therapist and hear it explained from a pragmatic viewpoint than to have it parroted with references "fore and aft."

The purpose of instruction and association with biblical truth is this: biblical truth as it touches upon life-experience represents responsible behavior. These truths are matters of precept. They are a necessary prerequisite to personality change, which takes place when biblical truth is ingested and incorporated into experience. And that is the next step in paracaletic therapy.

(2)Developing responsibility and rejecting irresponsibility:

Remember, involvement gives the therapist facility in effecting responsibility. Especially is this true of the procedure now under discussion. The therapist must earn the right to instruct or to encourage or to tell a patient that what he is doing is wrong.

One of the ministries of the Spirit of God is to comfort and encourage us. In his own way, he praises us for evidencing the fruit of the Spirit, and for things well done. His praise may come in the form of peace, overt joy and happiness, or quiet confidence and trust. One may say that he rewards responsible Christian experience and does not reward irresponsibility. It usually has its own reward.

The paracaletic therapist must assume the same posture. He must praise and reward good or responsible actions, beliefs, and attitudes of the patient, and reject irresponsibility by ignoring it or condemning it. However, the therapist must be careful that while condemning aspects of *behavior* he does not condemn the *person* doing it.

Gentle persuasion is usually the milieu for rejection of irresponsible behavior. But sometimes stronger, harsher measures must be taken. Sometimes a believer must be directly confronted with the reality and grave consequences of his irresponsibility. He must be made to see that what he is doing is wrong and sinful. In our opinion, this is where Adams's "nouthetic confrontation" finds its greatest validity.

This procedure of confrontation is the exception, not the rule. Jesus apparently followed it rarely. We are mindful of his searing words to Peter, "Get thee behind me, Satan, thou savourest not the things of God!" We also note that Paul socked it to Peter as well over the matter of legalism. This, in my view, is the admonishment spoken of in Scripture. It need not be this harsh and violent. It may simply assume the character of teaching or instruction. The *New American Standard Bible* translates *noutheteo* in this way. But it is didactic in form, not empathetic as is the case with *paracaleo*.

In the total process of involvement, responsibility, and encouragement and rejection, the therapist begins at a specific place on the *seven levels of responsibility* and works toward the seventh. A patient, in my view, cannot be considered cured until the therapist is certain that he is functioning normally at all levels.

WHEN TO REFER

Most ministers with the gift of counseling do not have the facilities for closed, in-patient therapy. It is a vision of the author to be instrumental in the establishment of a hospital staffed with paracaletic psychiatrists, psychologists, and medical personnel. Until that day comes, I must make referrals to men and institutions better prepared than I am to help such patients.

It is wise, if not imperative, to refer a prospective counselee to a medical doctor for a complete physical examination. No therapist must overlook the possibility that a patient's emotional problem may stem from a chemical imbalance or other physiological irregularity. If the patient has no family doctor, the therapist should have a doctor with whom he works or whom he could recommend for such an examination.

Personally, I believe that there are extremely few out-patient problems that a gifted minister or counselor could not treat paracaletically. But if a case presents itself which seems out of his field of competence, he most certainly should make a referral. His referral should be to someone in whom he has solid confidence. Sometimes, consultation with someone else of professional competence is to be preferred to referral. But if the patient is referred to someone in the psychiatric community, every effort must be made to insure that it is someone who generally follows the biblical principles of therapy. But be cautious. Many "Christian psychologists" are more "psychologist" than Christian in their therapeutic approach. If the basic biblical guidelines are not a controlling factor in their therapy, it is doubtful that they possess the spiritual gift of counseling, and it is unlikely that they would be any improvement over the minister himself.

Don't be too quick to refer. A counselor with a divine gift for counseling will rarely harm a patient, and the chances are good that he will help him. This is the general attitude of most psychologists who know nothing about God. If it is valid for them, certainly it must be valid for the person upon whom God has bestowed the gift of counseling. Remember that in the life of every human being, no matter what the degree of his aberration, God is sovereign and in control.

B: GROUP THERAPY AND SENSITIVITY TRAINING

Group therapy finds its value in both peer pressure and peer understanding and compassion. Alcoholics Anonymous and similar groups have been practicing it for years. The success of such groups bears dramatic testimony in support of the validity of the concept.

Group therapy will involve one or more therapists and a small group of people with either similar or differing problems. (There is value in discussion of both similar or dissimilar problems.) The therapist, hopefully, will not structure the sessions too heavily. He usually will prepare a general plan for discussion, but it is best not to be rigid in adhering to it unless there is ample reason for doing so.

The discussion follows the general rules for group dynamics. The therapist may direct a question to one member of the group who will respond, and a second member will be asked to comment on what the first has said. After initial awkwardness is forgotten, spontaneity takes over, and in time the therapist naturally becomes the coordinator of the discussion.

Member *A* is asked how he would handle a given problem. When he is finished, the other members are asked to comment or perhaps critize member *A's* analysis. Sometimes, discussion becomes heated. Verbal exchanges should not be discouraged, but deliberate attempts at insult or degrading attacks should be considered as irresponsible.

Again, involvement is the key. Only this time the members are trying to develop it among themselves, including the therapist. The beauty of Group Therapy is that it helps the patient to view himself through the eyes of others. After a few sessions of this, when the novelty of it has worn off, people generally become more candid with each other and real value results. The patient begins to see himself with a more objective perspective. He begins to see where he is, where he must go to meet his needs, and how far.

SENSITIVITY TRAINING

Sensitivity training has built into it the concept of a tactile relationship. Dr. Hawes (Chapter 3) supported this kind of relationship as a healthy influence in a society. We concur. If not encumbered with the excesses and abuses we read about in the tabloids, sensitivity training is a constructive therapeutic tool.

Tactile relationships were taken for granted in the New Testament. In some cases, it was part of ritual, e.g., the imposition of hands. Touching people is a very effective way to communicate one's affections for them. That this is true may be seen in a hurling fist or a lover's caress. Psychologists correctly tell us that the tactile relationship between a mother and her baby is an important need that we never really lose.

When he healed someone, Jesus very often touched him. Paul wrote of greeting one another with a holy kiss. Some may feel that Paul was following an oriental custom. I disagree. Some think it was a Christian ritual. I disagree. Peter referred to it as a kiss of love (1 Peter 5:14). In Christian circles, it must have been sincerely an expression of the love that one believer felt for another. We read of no male-female differentiation. We are left to conclude that the sex one happened to be made no difference. When Jesus entered the house of Simon, a woman "who was a sinner" (presumably a prostitute) fell down before him and wet his feet with her tears and began to kiss his feet. Simon objected *because she was a sinner.* Jesus remarked to Simon, "When I entered your home, you did not wash my feet; this woman has washed my feet with her tears. You gave me no kiss [implying that Simon should have], and this woman has not ceased to kiss my feet." Now unless we want to conclude that men kiss the head and that the feet are reserved for the women, we must assume that a kiss of love was a kiss of love, regardless of sex.

Of course, this type of expression of love among brothers and sisters in Christ is almost completely foreign in today's society. I'm not so sure but what we all are the losers.

The core, then, of sensitivity training is to help people to overcome a warped sense of propriety and an inability to express feeling. Initially or theoretically the whole thing may seem a bit artificial. It is suggested that a member of a Group Therapy gathering express his feelings toward another in the group without speaking and without physical harm. If genuine involvement has already been achieved, the expressions will be sincere. The subject to whom feelings are expressed may be asked not to respond, or he may be given freedom to respond—depending upon the objective of the session.

CLASSROOM THERAPY

One may wonder what kind of contribution a minister of the gospel can make to the field of education. While I haven't had an academic background in public education (other than being a student myself), I feel I can offer a few constructive comments. Perhaps being married to a very capable and sensitive schoolteacher causes me to be bold at this juncture. The principles of Love (paracaletic) Therapy can be of use in the schoolroom, and I would like to suggest how.

In an undeniable sense, a classroom should be an enlarged Group Therapy session. No one has more time to become involved with the students than does the teacher. Instead, he often views his role in a strictly didactic capacity. In my own experience, the classrooms where I learned the most were where the teacher dem-

onstrated sincere individual affection and concern for individual
learning.

The educational objective of the teacher for his students often
comes into conflict with the emotional and personal needs of both
himself and his students. I have seen teachers cry, scream, physi-
cally assault students, or leave the classroom in a fit of frustration.
Believe me, in most cases I sympathized with them. But such antics
point to one central malady: involvement has not been established.

In many cases, number of pupils, classroom facilities, and duration of exposure to each other have had a negative influence. It is
horribly unfortunate that lack of funds, or mismanagement of
funds, has contributed so magnificently to poor education. But
assuming these factors are pluses and not minuses; assuming a
teacher has all the necessary ingredients for a positive classroom
experience, the teacher should be an effective therapist to learning.

It is not the role of a teacher to perform the service of a book.
I have had a number of teachers and professors who have insulted
the intelligence of the students by reading from the text as a substi-
tute for a well-prepared lecture. The teacher does want to transmit
information, and I am convinced that the atmosphere in which that
objective is best accomplished is an atmosphere of involvement.
The teacher must view himself as the catalyst to learning. He is the
one who makes learning an exciting, stimulating experience. The
steps suggested in Chapter 18 for accomplishing involvement are
also valid for the classroom.

In my opinion, most classroom situations are far too structured.
There is too little use of group dynamics. If paracaletic therapy has
anything to commend it to the classroom situation, it is this: involvement is the key to communication of anything. It is the key
to responsible classroom behavior. Spend more time giving individual attention than time given to lesson plans. Determine to teach
in a relaxed, non-tense environment. These are mental postures and
can be achieved by a function of the will. Teach responsibility to
learning. Encourage good work. Don't make a big thing out of bad
work, but don't reward it.

BIBLIOGRAPHY

The following volumes represent works that have directly or indirectly influenced the author's viewpoint. This is not to say that he necessarily agrees with these books or any part of them, but they are offered as a background from which the present volume has been drawn. References recommended as particularly helpful in counseling and in formulating a Love Therapy mental attitude are indicated by an asterisk.

Adams, Jay E. *Competent to Counsel.* Presbyterian and Reformed Publishing Company, 1970.

Adolph, Paul E. *Release from Tension.* Chicago: Moody Press, 1956.

Allen, Charles L. *God's Psychiatry.* Westwood, New Jersey: Fleming H. Revell Company, 1953.

Banowsky, William S. *It's a Playboy World.* Old Tappan, New Jersey: Fleming H. Revell Company, 1969.

*Barkman, Paul F. *Man in Conflict.* Grand Rapids: Zondervan Publishing House, 1965.

Baruch, Dorothy W. *How to Live with Your Teenager.* New York: McGraw-Hill Book Company, Incorporated, 1953.

Bell, A. Donald. *The Family in Dialogue.* Grand Rapids: Zondervan Publishing House, 1968.

Birren, Faber. *Color Psychology and Color Therapy.* New Hyde Park, New York: University Books, Incorporated, 1961.

*Bonhoeffer, Dietrich. *Life Together.* New York: Harper and Row, Publishers, 1954.

Brandt, Henry R. and Dowdy, Homer E. *Building a Christian Home.* Wheaton: Scripture Press, 1960.

Brandt, Henry R. *The Struggle for Peace.* Wheaton: Scripture Press, Publications Incorporated, 1965.

Carnegie, Dale. *How to Win Friends and Influence People.* Simon and Schuster, 1936.

Carothers, Merlin. *Prison to Praise.* Plainfield, New Jersey: Logos International, 1970.

Chafer, Louis Sperry. *Systematic Theology.* Dallas: Dallas Seminary Press, 1948.

*Christenson, Larry. *The Christian Family.* Minneapolis: Bethany Fellowship, Incorporated, 1970.

Collins, Gary. *Search for Reality.* Wheaton: Key Publishers, 1969.

*Crim, Mort. *Like it Is!* Anderson, Indiana: The Warner Press, 1970.

De Laszio, Violet Staub. (ed.) *The Basic Writings of C. G. Jung.* New York: The Modern Library, 1959.

*Dobson, James. *Dare to Discipline.* Wheaton: Tyndale House Publishers, 1970.

*Draper, Edgar. *Psychiatry and Pastoral Care.* Englewood Cliffs, New Jersey: Prentice-Hall, Incorporated, 1965.

Edman, V. Raymond. *The Disciplines of Life.* Minneapolis: World Wide Publications, 1948.

*Eichenlaub, John E. *The Marriage Art.* New York: The Dell Publishing Company, 1961.

Ellenberger, Henri F. *The Discovery of the Unconscious.* New York: Basic Books, Incorporated, 1970.

Fromm, Erich. *Psychoanalysis and Religion.* New Haven and London: Yale University Press, 1950.

Geldenhuys, Norval. *The Intimate Life.* Grand Rapids: William B. Eerdman's Publishing Company, 1957.

*Gillquist, Peter E. *Love Is Now.* Grand Rapids: Zondervan Publishing House, 1970.

*Ginott, Haim G. *Between Parent and Child.* New York: McGraw-Hill Book Company, Incorporated, 1961.

*_____. *Between Parent and Teenager.* New York: The Macmillan Company, 1969.

*Glasser, William. *Mental Health or Mental Illness.* New York: Harper and Row, Publishers, 1960.

*_____. *Schools Without Failure.* New York: Harper and Row, Publishers, 1969.

*_____. *Reality Therapy.* New York: Harper and Row, Publishers, 1965.

Guntrip, Harry. *Healing the Sick Mind.* New York: Appleton Century, 1964.

Halverson, Richard C. *Between Sundays.* Grand Rapids: Zondervan Publishing House, 1965.

_____. *Man to Man.* Grand Rapids: Zondervan Publishing House, 1961.

Hebb, Donald Olding. *A Textbook of Psychology.* Philadelphia: W. B. Saunders Company, 1966.

Herrnstein, Richard J. and Boring, Edwin G. *A Source Book in the History of Psychology.* Cambridge: Harvard University Press, 1965.

Hill, Napoleon. *Grow Rich!—With Peace of Mind.* Greenwich, Connecticut: Fawcett Publications, 1967.

_____. *Think and Grow Rich.* Greenwich, Connecticut: Fawcett Publications, 1967.

*Hodge, Marshall Bryant. *Your Fear of Love.* Garden City, New York: Doubleday and Company, Incorporated, 1967.

*Howard, Thomas. *Christ the Tiger.* Philadelphia: J. B. Lippincott Company, 1967.

Hunt, Gladys. *Listen to Me!* Downers Grove, Illinois: Inter Varsity Press, 1969.

*Hyder, O. Quentin. *The Christian Handbook of Psychiatry.* Old Tappan, New Jersey: Fleming H. Revell Company, 1971.

*Kirby, Clyde. *Then Came Jesus.* Grand Rapids: Zondervan Publishing House, 1967.

LaHaye, Tim. *Spirit-Controlled Temperament.* Wheaton: Tyndale House Publishers, 1966.

*_____. *Transformed Temperaments.* Wheaton: Tyndale House Publishers, 1971.

*Link, Martin. *He Is the Still Point of the Turning World.* Chicago: Argus Communications, 1971.

Little, L. Gilbert. *Nervous Christians.* Chicago: Moody Press, 1956.

*Luscher, Max. *The Luscher Color Test.* Ian A. Scott (ed.) New York: Random House Publishers, 1969.

Maltz, Maxwell. *Creative Living for Today.* Trident Press, 1967.

_____. *Psycho-Cybernetics.* Englewood Cliffs, New Jersey: Prentice-Hall Publishers, 1960.

*May, Rollo. *The Art of Counseling.* New York: The Abingdon Press, 1967.

McMillan, S. I. *None of These Diseases.* Old Tappan, New Jersey: Fleming H. Revell Company, MCMLXIII.

*Miles, Herbert J. *Sexual Happiness in Marriage.* Grand Rapids: Zondervan Publishing House, 1967.

*Mulder, Jacob D. *Psychiatry for Pastors, Students and Nurses.* Grand Rapids: Wm. B. Eerdman's Publishing Company, 1939.

Munn, Norman L. *Psychology: The Fundamentals of Human Adjustment.* Boston: Houghton Mifflin Company, 1966.

*Narramore, Clyde M. *Encyclopedia of Psychological Problems.* Grand Rapids: Zondervan Publishing House, 1966.

_____. *The Psychology of Counseling.* Grand Rapids: Zondervan Publishing House, 1960.

_____. *Young Only Once.* Grand Rapids: Zondervan Publishing House, 1957.

Olford, Stephen F. and Lawes, Frank A. *The Sanctity of Sex.* Westwood, New Jersey: Fleming H. Revell Company, MCMLXIII.

Orwell, George. *1984.* The New American Library, 1949.

Peale, Norman Vincent. *The Power of Positive Thinking.* Englewood Cliffs, New Jersey: Prentice-Hall Publishers, 1952.

*Petersen, Allan J. (ed.) *The Marriage Affair.* Wheaton: Tyndale House Publishers, 1971.

Pinckney, Edward R., and Pinckney, Cathy. *The Fallacy of Freud and Psychoanalysis.* Englewood Cliffs, New Jersey: Prentice-Hall, Incorporated, 1963.

Powell, John. *Why Am I Afraid to Love?* Chicago: Argus Communications Company, 1967.

Pressey, Sidney L., Robinson, Francis P., and Horrocks, John E. *Psychology in Education.* New York: Harper and Brothers Publishers, 1933.

Rogers, Carl. *Encounter Groups.* New York: Harper and Row Publishers, 1970.

*Ryrie, Charles Caldwell. *Balancing the Christian Life.* Chicago: Moody Press, 1969.

_____. *Dispensationalism Today.* Chicago: Moody Press, 1965.

_____. *The Basis for Premillennial Faith.* Neptune, New Jersey: Loizeaux Brothers, 1953.

Schaeffer, Francis A. *The God Who Is There.* Chicago: Inter Varsity Press, 1968.

_____. *The Mark of a Christian.* Chicago: Inter Varsity Press, 1968.

Shelly, Bruce. *Let's Face It.* Chicago: Moody Press, 1968.

Shepard, Martin, and Lee, Marjorie. *Games Analysts Play.* New York: G. P. Putnam's Sons, 1970.

Small, Dwight Harvey. *Design for Christian Marriage.* Old Tappan, New Jersey: Fleming H. Revell Company MCMLIX

Smith, A. E. Wilder. *The Drug Users.* Wheaton: Harold Shaw Publishers, 1969.

Strunk, Orlo Jr. *Mature Religion, A Psychological Study.* New York: Abingdon Press, 1965.

Toffler, Alvin. *Future Shock.* New York: Random House Publishers, 1970.

Webber, Robert. (Compiler) *Rappings.* Wheaton: Tyndale House Publishers, 1971.

Woodworth, Robert S., and Sheehan, Mary R. *Contemporary Schools of Psychology.* New York: The Ronald Press Company, 1964.

Zilboorg, Gregory. *A History of Medical Psychology.* New York: W. W. Morton Company, 1941.